BUILD A BETTER
ORGANIZATION

BUILD A BETTER
ORGANIZATION

How Effective Leadership and Strong Culture
Can Create a High-Performance Organization

ROBERT J. KOHLHEPP

Aamass Publishing LLC
Cincinnati, OH

Published by
Aamass Publishing LLC | Cincinnati, OH

Publisher's Cataloging-in-Publication Data
Kohlhepp, Robert J.

Build a better organization : how effective leadership and strong culture can create a high-performance organization / by Robert J. Kohlhepp. – Cincinnati, Ohio : Aamass Pub. LLC, 2021.

p. ; cm.

ISBN13: 978-0-9601091-0-4

1. Organizational behavior. 2. Leadership. 3. Corporate culture. 4. Personnel management. I. Title.

HD58.7.K64 2021
302.35--dc23

Project coordination by Jenkins Group, Inc. | www.jenkinsgroupinc.com

Special thanks to Marcia Layton Turner for her help drafting this book.

Interior design by Brooke Camfield

Printed in the United States of America
25   24   23   22   21   •   5   4   3   2   1

DEDICATION

To my wife, Linda, and our children, Brent, Scott, and Becky. You made my career and journey possible with your love, understanding, and support.

And to Dick and Scott Farmer. Without Dick's mentoring, tenacity, and leadership, the Cintas story wouldn't have happened. Dick handed me the baton to run the company, and I handed it to Scott, who has continued the company legacy of excellence admirably.

CONTENTS

FOREWORD   ix
PREFACE   xiii
INTRODUCTION   xv

PART I: *CULTURE*   1
CHAPTER 1: *DETERMINING YOUR PRINCIPAL OBJECTIVE*   3
CHAPTER 2: *DEFINING YOUR CORPORATE CHARACTER*   17
CHAPTER 3: *ESTABLISHING MANAGEMENT SYSTEMS*   31
CHAPTER 4: BASIC ETHICS   45

PART II: *PEOPLE*   57
CHAPTER 5: *HIRING THE RIGHT PEOPLE*   59
CHAPTER 6: *MANAGING PEOPLE EFFECTIVELY*   73
CHAPTER 7: *HOLDING ON TO YOUR BEST PEOPLE*   87

PART III: *LEADERSHIP*   99
CHAPTER 8: *THE NINE CHARACTERISTICS OF GREAT LEADERS*   101
CHAPTER 9: *BEING TOUGH*   115
CHAPTER 10: *LEARNING FROM MISTAKES*   127
CHAPTER 11: *HAVING HIGH EXPECTATIONS*   135

EPILOGUE   145
ABOUT THE AUTHOR   151
INDEX   153

FOREWORD

When Bob Kohlhepp called and asked if I would consider writing the foreword to his new book, it was an offer I couldn't refuse. Bob and I worked together for a decade as members of the Board of Trustees of Xavier University, where I had the pleasure of witnessing firsthand his skills as a leader—Bob was Xavier's board chair for most of that period—and his forthrightness and sincerity as a person. Reading *Build a Better Organization*, I quickly realized that Bob had put into practice at Xavier many of the tenets that led to his business success with Cintas.

Like most business executives, I've read a goodly number of business books. Inevitably, someone is touting a new way of managing, a new path to success, or some disruptive this or that. Bob reminds us that successful businesses are and always will be built by the application of a handful of fundamental principles and practices, along with the discipline to execute these effectively. *Build a Better Organization* provides the reader with a how-to guide against which to judge the operational effectiveness of any enterprise.

Culture. People. Leadership.

These must be the pivotal areas of focus within any organization that seeks to thrive and prosper in the long run. Attention to these three critical determinants of success propelled Cintas to become one of the great American business success stories of recent times—and with more to come, I expect. Through the use of anecdotes and experiences gained from his five decades of service to the company, Bob brings to life the do's and don'ts that apply equally to the first-line supervisor, the general manager, and the CEO; principles that apply to enterprises large or small: ones grown from the ground up like Cintas or established centenarians like the enterprise I was privileged to lead, Eli Lilly and Company.

With his career at Cintas as the background for this book, Bob provides the reader with a unique opportunity to witness a company move from the start-up stage to its present standing in the Fortune 500. He describes how many of the business practices and ways of working at Cintas developed out of necessity as the company grew, for example, the importance of gaining alignment around the core purpose of the business and the way its leaders wish to see it operate. This is a challenge for any company of significant size, regardless of longevity. In my experience, Bob's emphasis on communicating (and then communicating again, and then again), engaging with frontline employees, and seeking employee input and encouraging new ideas are critical success factors for any enterprise.

As a CEO, I learned firsthand the veracity of so many of Bob's precepts. Chief among them is the overarching importance of people and the absolute requirement to hire great people, to motivate and reward them, to develop them and provide them with an opportunity to grow. Careful attention to people—partners, in Cintas parlance—invariably pays the dividends that enable a business to delight customers and succeed in a way that rewards shareholders and so many others, including suppliers and local communities. I marvel, for example, at the attention paid by Cintas managers to the hiring process and to performance evaluation. As I observed in my own working years, no single person is indispensable, but it's amazing how one person—the right person for the job—can make an incredible difference. I saw this time and again.

As much as *Build a Better Organization* is about organizational effectiveness, it has much to say about the qualities and characteristics required of the men and women who are tasked with leading the organization. In today's business world, the ability to create a climate that encourages individuals to speak up and to bring forward their concerns, as well as their ideas, is essential. The culture of any enterprise—for better or worse—is ultimately set by the "tone at the top." The strong Cintas culture, rooted in professionalism, has developed and strengthened because of the foresight, the courage, and the discipline exhibited by Bob Kohlhepp and his colleagues for over half a century. We are fortunate in these pages to learn and benefit from their story.

John C. Lechleiter
Retired Chairman and CEO
Eli Lilly and Company

PREFACE

During my 50 years at Cintas, I did a lot of teaching, both inside and outside of the company. Much of that teaching was focused on the importance of culture within an organization, the role of leadership, and the opportunity to share my experiences of working for and building a great company that was so successful. After many of these sessions, people would tell me that I should write a book. I thought about it for a long time but, for many reasons, never moved forward.

Then one day I received a book in the mail from one of the principals of a private equity company on whose board of directors I still serve. The book was entitled *Trillion Dollar Coach* and was about a man named Bill Campbell who had mentored several executives in Silicon Valley, including Steve Jobs; it was written by three people Campbell had mentored. Enclosed with the book was a note from my colleague saying he thought I would enjoy the book because he knew I had mentored the president of a company we had invested in for several years and because he felt I had a significant impact on the young man, much like Campbell had on his mentees.

I read the book from cover to cover in just a few days. Reading it and hearing about the tremendous impact Campbell had on so many people inspired me to write this book, in the hopes that I might have even a fraction of the impact that he did. My goal was to share all the experiences I had through the years, to help others run better companies and organizations, to help them learn how to hire the right people, and to be better managers and motivators of the people who work for them and with them.

One of the things that I believe I did right was finding an organization that matched my own values and work ethic and that provided me the opportunity to grow with it, just as Dick Farmer, Cintas's founder, had hoped. I joined the business as a 23-year-old with a few years of accounting and customer service experience, choosing to leave my current employer because I saw the huge potential that Cintas offered. Thanks to Dick's ability to share his vision for the company, I could see how it could grow, what it would need to do to achieve his goals, and how my skills could play a role.

Partnering with an organization committed to being the best in its industry was a great way to spend the career of a lifetime.

Robert J. Kohlhepp
February 8, 2021

INTRODUCTION

Being able to spend nearly 50 years of my career at one company was an accomplishment, especially in modern times. The fact that those 50 years were spent at Cintas, one of the best-run companies I know, was a blessing. During my time there, I learned about how to build a company, how to hire the right people, how to manage and lead people, how to achieve results ethically and fairly, and so much more. Thanks to the opportunity to work with many great leaders, and in particular Dick Farmer, who started Cintas, and Father Jim Hoff, who led Xavier University, I saw firsthand what it looked like to lead with integrity.

When I joined Cintas in 1967 as its controller, company sales had hit $1.6 million, with $15,000 in profits, assets of $784,000, and only 62 employees. It was still in the early stages of growth. Fast-forward to 2020, when Cintas had $7.1 billion in sales, $876 million in profits, assets of $7.7 billion, and more than 40,000 employees. The transformation I had the privilege of witnessing during my time there was incredible.

HISTORY OF CINTAS

Year	Sales	Net Income	Assets
1967	$1,603,000	$15,000	$784,000
1977	$18,297,000	$1,181,000	$10,108,000
1987	$163,375,000	$13,936,000	$161,844,000
1997	$839,949,000	$89,490,000	$761,823,000
2007	$3,706,900,000	$334,538,000	$3,570,480,000
2017	$5,400,000,000	$500,000,000	$4,271,164,000
2020	$7,085,000,000	$876,000,000	$7,669,885,000
50 Year Cpd Growth	18.0%	23.4%	19.8%

THE RIGHT PLACE AT THE RIGHT TIME

Unlike many young hires, I didn't join Cintas straight out of college. I had skipped two grades in middle school—seventh and eighth grades, to be exact—and started high school at age 11. I graduated from high school at age 15 and started college then, graduating as a 19-year-old. I was a practicing CPA in an accounting firm with four years of experience when my name came up as a candidate for a controller role that Dick Farmer was looking to fill at Cintas.

Dick had been advised to hire young college graduates to fill some of his new management roles, so that they could grow with the job and the company. That made sense to him, especially as he had found that many of his new hires without degrees did a fine job, but only up to a point. After several months they really needed training in order to progress. Dick had decided that he'd rather hire people who had the potential to grow with the company. So he tapped into his professional network to start to identify young college graduates who might be strong additions to the Cintas team. He made a number of phone calls to friends and colleagues to spread the word that he was looking for young high performers to hire.

As Dick was beginning his search for future management candidates, I was working as a CPA, often alongside attorneys. One attorney who shared some mutual clients was Don Klekamp. Don was one of the people in Dick's network, so he was aware that Dick was looking for new talent. And it just so happened that after having a conversation with Dick, Don and I had a client meeting during which I apparently said something insightful that impressed Don. Right after the meeting, Don called Dick with news.

"Dick, I have someone whom I'm very impressed with, and since you mentioned you're looking for a new controller who is a young college graduate, I think you ought to talk to him," Don told him.

"How old is he?" Dick asked.

"He's 23 years old," Don told him.

"Gee, 23 is really young," Dick replied. "I mean, young is one thing, but 23 is just too young, I think. He must have just graduated from college. I think I'll pass."

About three weeks later, Don and I had another meeting with another mutual client, and I guess I said something else that impressed Don, which inspired him to call Dick back to encourage him to speak with me. "Dick, you've really got to talk to this guy," he said. "I know he's only 23, but he sure doesn't act like he's 23."

So one day I received a call from Dick, who told me, "I've heard about you, and I'm looking for a controller. I wonder if you'd talk to me about it," he asked.

"Dick, I'm very happy where I am, and I have no interest, but thank you for the call," I told him.

That did not dissuade Dick one bit. He is an extremely persistent person, and he kept calling me asking for a meeting. He wore me down, I'll admit. So when he said, "What's the harm in just meeting with me and talking?" I agreed. Why not?

I noticed immediately after meeting him that Dick had tremendous enthusiasm and determination. He was inspiring. He told me he wanted to take his little company and build it into a national company and, in the process, become financially independent. That caught my attention. Although I've never solely worked for money, or used it as a gauge for success the way some other people do, financial independence meant that you could control your own destiny. Someone who is financially independent can do whatever they want to do; they don't have anything or anyone else determining their fate. That was very appealing to me.

He made me an offer.

I didn't jump at the opportunity immediately. In fact, I had a hard time making up my mind. I went back to the accounting firm I worked for and told them about the offer. Because I was someone they considered an up-and-comer in the firm, they didn't want me to go, and I wasn't convinced I wanted to leave. So I went to church and knelt in the pew, asking for God's guidance. After two hours, I knew what he wanted me to do.

I called Dick and asked him when he'd like me to start. That's how my career at Cintas began.

RISING IN THE RANKS

From the controller position, I was promoted to chief financial officer, then vice president and treasurer, and then I became president, chief operating officer, and, finally, CEO. After that I was vice chairman and retired in 2016 as chairman of the board.

In each of those roles, I took away something new about how to build an organization and better manage people. I learned so much from the terrific managers around me, and I tried to put that knowledge to good use as I managed others.

My best decision by far, however, was in choosing the company to work for, and I strongly advise you to invest the same amount of time in scoping out any organization you intend to work with.

Find one that matches your values and morals and that rewards the kind of good work you have a passion for. If you do that, both you and your employer will benefit immeasurably.

PART I
CULTURE

You can hire the best talent, invest in the best equipment, and serve the best customers, but unless you create a corporate culture that is satisfied only with excellence, your efforts will fail.

To build a great organization, you need to first determine your principal objective—your reason for being, or your mission. Unified by that guiding mission, you can foster a culture dedicated to excellence, customer satisfaction, and employee engagement.

In addition to defining your corporate objective, you also need to establish your organization's corporate character, or the central values and philosophy that will drive decisions from the top.

Developing management systems and processes that ensure that customers receive the same high level of service they have come to expect is critical for consistency. And, finally, establishing an understanding of what ethical behavior looks like within your organization sets parameters for how things should be done.

Together, those elements shape your organization's internal and external reputations—how you are perceived, based on how you treat employees, suppliers, customers, and your community. It all goes back to culture. And culture determines how successful you will be as a company, agency, or nonprofit.

CHAPTER 1

DETERMINING YOUR PRINCIPAL OBJECTIVE

Guided by a principal objective, or a singular mission, average companies can achieve great things. Jim Collins made that point in *Good to Great*, James Clear stated it in *Atomic Habits*, and Gary Keller covered it in *The One Thing*. Determining that one core mission your organization will strive to achieve can be like a lightning bolt that unifies everyone's efforts.

That was certainly true at Cintas, which was steadfast in its commitment to maintaining and nurturing its corporate culture. A big part of that corporate culture was our principal objective—that one statement against which all decisions were evaluated. Together with our corporate character and management system, those three elements made up our corporate culture.

At the heart of our culture was our people, or our partners, as we preferred to call them. Only through their efforts could Cintas achieve its principal objective—which is why it was quite concerning when a few managers elected to leave the company back in the mid-1970s. That was unusual. Cintas's retention rate for management people had always been well over 90 percent, and then-CEO Dick Farmer was wary that a pattern might be emerging.

To try to get to the root of why these people were leaving, Dick called a Saturday morning meeting in his office. Although working on Saturdays was typical at Cintas, an official meeting was not, signaling to us that this was a big deal. There were four of us in the room: the CEO, Dick Farmer; the head of the rental division, Joe Detzel; the head of human resources, Bill Miller; and me. We were all focused on identifying what was causing the sudden uptick in defections and deciding what, if anything, we should do to address it.

We started by making a list of who had left in the past few years and then dug into why they quit or were let go. We discussed the circumstances under which Joe left. Then we talked about Mary, then Pete, and on down our list of seven or eight former management staff members. We discussed each one in considerable detail, trying to discern why they elected to leave when they did or why we had felt it necessary to let them go. Was there anything these individuals had in common? we wondered. Then Bill Miller, the director of human resources, spoke up.

"Well, you know, most of these people weren't a culture fit," he said.

"What do you mean by 'culture fit,' Bill?" we asked, curious about his statement.

Then he explained, "We do things differently, and that didn't work for everyone. For example, we work Saturdays, and some of these people on the list didn't. They may have joined us from bigger companies that didn't work Saturdays, and they didn't want to give up that time." He continued, "Because of our size, we do a lot of things ourselves. That's harder for people used to working with a huge support staff. We don't have that. We're also pretty intense. We take goals and objectives seriously, and we have a sense of urgency about our work—a faster pace—that not everyone can adjust to," he said. "We're also honest and direct in how we communicate; we don't sugarcoat things. We face tough situations head-on rather than avoid them. Not everyone appreciates that or is comfortable with that level of honesty and frankness," he said. "We also take our commitments seriously. We do what we say we're going to do."

We sat in silence for a couple of minutes, processing this observation.

In fact, Bill had just articulated the Cintas culture. And he was right: the people who had moved on to other job opportunities had not embraced or appreciated the type of work environment that had emerged within the company.

We also recognized that their departures were our fault; some of those individuals shouldn't have been hired in the first place. As senior leaders, we had done a poor job of defining and articulating our corporate culture to our partners and employment candidates. Without that clear vision of how we wanted our organization to function, it was almost impossible to assess the compatibility of prospective employees. We hadn't been fair to them, we realized.

Until that moment, we hadn't taken the time to define our culture. Inspired by this fact, we proceeded to write a short book, titled *The Spirit Is the Difference*, which was spearheaded by Dick, to do just that: define, describe, and disseminate the Cintas culture.

The book was useful in a number of ways, by providing a brief history of the company and describing what it was like to work at Cintas and what was important to us as an organization. More important, it also served as a road map for all of our partners regarding how they were expected to act and dress and conduct business. It crystallized for everyone what it meant to work at Cintas.

DETERMINING OUR PRINCIPAL OBJECTIVE

Although every organization has a culture that is the product of the people, their attitudes and behaviors, and the priorities of senior leadership, very few organizations formalize that culture by committing it to writing. We wanted to capture our ideal culture on paper so that we could continue to foster its development within Cintas.

The first element of our culture, our principal objective, defined how decisions should be made. It made clear what our priority was—customer satisfaction—as well as our desired outcome—maximizing long-term value for our shareholders and working partners.

We will exceed our customers' expectations to maximize
the long-term value of Cintas for its shareholders
and working partners.
                                        —Cintas's principal objective

Having a principal objective simplified decision-making. Rather than considering multiple factors or desired results and weighing many potential outcomes, we only had to consider which approach would result in exceeding customer expectations and maximizing long-term value for shareholders and partners.

Using that one sentence as the measuring stick, we found that solutions became crystal clear. Should we buy a particular company? Only if it will aid our ability to exceed customer expectations and maximize value. Should we enter a new market? Only if it will allow us to better serve our customers and continue to exceed their expectations. Should we hire or fire someone? That answer depended on whether the individual was contributing or could contribute to our ability to exceed customer expectations. Should we modify salary levels? Only if it would contribute to our ability to exceed customer expectations.

This sentence, our principal objective, drove every corporate decision.

WHO IS THE MOST IMPORTANT CONSTITUENT?

When I led the corporate culture discussion for new management partners, I always asked them which of the three constituents mentioned in our principal objective was the most important. We mention customers first, with shareholders and working partners being rewarded if we serve that first audience well. But should customers be our sole focus? And what about our other constituents, such as our community, our environment, and our suppliers?

The common dilemma faced by every management team is addressing how you keep the majority of your customers, shareholders, and working partners satisfied. There is often a conflict that may preclude satisfying all three constituents simultaneously, so can it be done?

When I asked partners in the class to prioritize Cintas's three constituents, I most often heard that satisfying our customers should be our primary goal. Some class participants made the case that satisfying our shareholders was most important, while others felt that our partners were the key.

They were right. Happy and satisfied partners produce happy and satisfied customers, which produce happy and satisfied shareholders. Partners were really the driving force.

Finding, hiring, and keeping partners has rarely been an issue, except when we discover the lack of the previously mentioned culture fit.

HANDLING CULTURE SHOCK

We became well aware of how important culture was in evaluating potential acquisition candidates. In many cases, it was blatantly obvious which companies had cultures that were in alignment with Cintas's and which had those where a great deal of adjustment would be needed. We called that "culture shock."

We explained that culture shock was a lot like what pro athletes feel when they've been traded from the team where they've played for years to an entirely different team. You know walking in that it's likely that they operate differently from your last team. The drills on the field will be different, the coaching approach will be different, the uniforms will be different, and the procedures during practice will be different.

So we explained to employees joining us from other organizations that they would likely experience culture shock, and that was OK. We would say, "We don't expect you to flip a switch and in a matter of days be completely familiar and compatible with our culture and our values. It will take time for you to understand why we have those values, how they manifest themselves, and how we expect you to operate. Fortunately, your boss will help you with that transition."

Then I would always tell them, "After about a year, you should be able to decide for yourself whether you want to get on the bus or get off. Because if you can't operate in compatibility with the majority of our values, then you won't be successful here. You won't be promoted, and you'll likely be frustrated. And that's when it's probably time for you to go work somewhere else, where you'll be better off." My goal wasn't to discourage them but to alert them that within several months, they should be able to decide for themselves whether they felt a part of the Cintas team or not. And if not, we'd help them find an employer that was a better fit for them.

We also learned that the older you were, the harder it was to adapt to our culture. Or if you joined us from a company with a very different culture, it was doubly hard. Over time, we started to identify certain organizations—many of them very well known and some well respected—that had a culture too different from that of Cintas. And we vowed not to hire anyone from those companies, because it was just too difficult for them to adjust.

Part of the problem in some of the organizations was that the boss at the top was setting the standard. They seemed to have forgotten that everyone looks to the CEO for clues regarding what is acceptable and what is not. Whatever the boss does, they're going to emulate. That's true whether the boss is showing up late to meetings, using curse words in their communication, or coming to work in sweatpants. The boss conveys what is acceptable and what is not.

STORYTELLING AS CULTURAL INDOCTRINATION

Realizing the importance of conveying the company's culture to every current and future partner, we began holding half-day corporate culture seminars for new management employees. We used *The Spirit as the Difference* as our textbook of sorts, and we worked to really bring that book to life for everyone in that day's session through stories. It's one thing to read about a particular policy and quite another to hear about that policy in action.

During these sessions, we shared story after story about situations with customers and how we addressed them, to demonstrate best practices and help partners understand the factors we wanted them to consider as they thought through how best to deal with conflicts that arose. In all cases, the decisions came down to what would exceed expectations for that customer—not the cost or the inconvenience to us, but to what degree a particular solution would satisfy and delight that customer.

FOSTERING A "CULTLIKE CULTURE"

In *Built to Last*, Jim Collins reported that the top companies in all the industries he studied stood out by having "a cultlike culture." Within each company, everyone looked the same, acted the same, and functioned the same.

That was what we at Cintas strove for: complete harmony.

I remember playing golf with a couple of our competitors several years ago at a trade association conference. I was in the cart with one of our competitors, and he turned, looked me up and down, and said, "You know, you guys are like a school of fish."

Confused, I asked what he meant by that comment.

He responded, "Well, the head turns one way, and all thousand of you have to go in the same direction. It drives us crazy!"

I took it as a compliment, or at least a sign that we were doing a good job of communicating our culture throughout the organization.

In the culture seminar that I'd help lead, I typically used a boat analogy to explain culture. "Every organization is like a boat," I would say. "And in that boat you have a bunch of different people. Each of those people has an oar. In many organizations, half the people are rowing in one direction, and the other half rowing in another. They don't make much progress forward. But when you can get a majority of the people in the organization—not even all of them, but a majority—rowing in the same direction, the progress made is so much faster than any other organization. They become a united force few other companies can compete with, because they have a single goal everyone is working together to achieve."

When you had people who were working in their own best interest but not the company's, that was a sign that they were not aligned with

Cintas's principal objective. I remember one situation involving a plant manager who was not rowing in sync with his other partners or with the company.

The situation arose out of our need for growth. Dick and I had had many conversations about the optimal size of a plant. When we began outgrowing a plant, meaning demand was exceeding capacity, we'd have discussions about where to locate another plant that could relieve the pressure on the existing plant. Dick had originally argued in favor of building bigger plants, what he called "megaplants," but after talking through the advantages and disadvantages of a huge plant versus multiple smaller plants, he was in favor of more, smaller plants. The advantage was that most plant managers could get to know up to 200 people under their roof—but grow beyond 200 partners and it became nearly impossible. So we put a ceiling of 200 employees on our plants.

When we reached maximum capacity at our plant in Houston many years ago, I approached Bob, the manager there, for his advice on where we should locate a second plant. He was dead set against the idea. "I don't think this is the right thing to do," he told me. "I helped build this company. I took it from a very small company, and now we're doing $20 million at this location. And you want to split it in half, and I can run only half of it? I just don't think that's right."

I explained all the reasons we needed a second location, which included being more centrally located for the customer base around it, being able to staff it with partners who knew the local customer base, and providing additional production capability. Bob still didn't think it was fair to him.

So I pulled out our principal objective and asked him to read it. "Do you see your name in there anywhere?" I asked him.

There was dead silence for 30 seconds as he pondered the question while looking at the sheet of paper.

"I guess I don't," he slowly responded.

"Bob, we're not making these decisions based on what's best for you or what's best for me or even what's best for Dick Farmer," I told him.

"We're making these decisions based on what's best for all of our customers, all of our shareholders, and all of our employees, which is what this principal objective says."

"All right, I got it," he said. And he really did. He demonstrated that he understood why we considered him, and each of the people we work with, a partner.

In another situation, somewhat similar, we were looking for locations for a second plant. The general manager of the original plant, who was going to move to run the new plant, was pushing hard for the plant to be located in a certain area. We checked it out and just couldn't see the advantage of that particular site, so we asked him to make a case for it, since its advantages weren't clear.

It turns out it was great because it was 5–10 minutes from his home, so his commute would be much shorter if it were built there.

Again, I had to pull out the principal objective and ask him where he was mentioned, because we weren't building the plant according to what was best or most convenient for him. It was our customers we were focused on serving.

Other times we would marvel at what other companies did, supposedly in service to their customers. Our facilities, for example, were designed to be spartan but professional. We wanted them clean and neat and tastefully decorated, but we didn't spend tens of thousands of dollars outfitting our workspaces.

In contrast, we were shocked to hear that the former CEO of Tyco had spent $100 million on fine art to hang on the walls at the company headquarters. We couldn't quite imagine how a CEO could justify spending so lavishly on something that wouldn't benefit the company's customers at all. It's one thing to spend your own salary on fine art for your home, but spending company money on assets that couldn't help us achieve our principal objective was inconceivable to us.

We would rather invest money in training or rewarding our partners.

REWARDING OUR PARTNERS

The term "partner" was actually coined by Bruce Rotte, a gentleman who ran one of our rental groups. At Cintas, we had long referred to our workforce as employees, though we didn't think it reflected the importance of each individual to the business. We didn't like the word "associate," though many companies adopted the term. So when I heard Bruce refer to the people in his group as partners, we asked him about it.

"Well, our employees are our partners. We're all in this together," he said. And he was right.

Before we switched to using the term "partner," however, we decided that we really needed to make our employees partners. That led us, in 1971, to create the Cintas Partners' Plan—the company's retirement plan—which initially consisted of a profit-sharing plan and 401(k) plan. Since 1983, after we went public, each year Cintas has also contributed company stock into the Partners' Plan.

What was different about Cintas's plan was how employee credits in the program were earned. We credited employees on both salary and years of service. In contrast, many company retirement plans base contributions strictly on compensation. Our goal was to make it possible for employees at all levels of the company to retire comfortably, and the Cintas Partners Plan has done that for many, many employees.

Every employee of the company was truly a full-fledged partner in the company from then on, except for the few union employees who had their own retirement plan as part of the union contract. These partners became owners in the company, which aligned their interests with the interest of other shareholders and our customers.

In addition to driving home the importance of every single contributor on our payroll, giving partners an ownership stake in the company changed their mindset. Their concern for how money is spent increased, because they understood that money wasted affects the value of the stock held in the employee stock ownership plan. They became even more committed to making the company—*their* company—successful. It was magical.

DEVELOPING AN EFFECTIVE PRINCIPAL OBJECTIVE

Every organization should have its own principal objective, that short sentence, or two, that guides decision-making.

At Cintas, we had three major constituents: customers, shareholders, and partners. And with each big decision to be made, we would sit down and assess how it would achieve the principal objective. We would think through the "what-ifs." That is, what if we take this action? How does it maximize the long-term value of our company, shareholders, and working partners, and how does it exceed our customers' expectations? We would evaluate the impact of any decision on each of our three major constituents and confirm that it would support our principal objective before proceeding.

There is a big difference between writing a principal objective and living it, however. Just look at Enron's vision statement pre-implosion: "Enron's vision is to become the world's leading energy company— creating innovative and efficient energy solutions for growing economies and a better environment worldwide." That sounds clear, even noble, but without any indication of *how* the company would achieve that vision, its employees turned to unethical and even illegal means.

Before its collapse, Lehman Brothers' mission statement also sounded respectable: "Our mission is to build unrivaled partnerships with and value for our clients, through the knowledge, creativity, and dedication of our people, leading to superior results for our shareholders." It sounded good, but the majority of employees didn't actually follow through in applying those promises to the company's operations.

It's a lot like going on a diet. You can proclaim an intent to eat better, exercise regularly, and drink lots of water, but the hard part is actually doing those things. Choosing to make better choices at meals, reducing snacking, trading water for coffee or wine—those are times where it's easy for people to fall down.

That's what happens at many companies. Senior leadership will write a principal objective representing what the company is striving for that has no basis in reality. Sure, it sounds good, but the majority of companies don't actually live it.

At Cintas, we drilled that principal objective into our team repeatedly. We started by communicating it clearly and frequently to every new working partner. Then we sent managers to our half-day seminar to learn about it and talk about it, to clear up any questions about how the principal objective should be applied. But most importantly, we empowered our partners to point out when other partners weren't behaving in alignment with that objective—meaning we asked anyone in the company to confront anyone else who was doing anything out of sync with our culture. We made it an obligation to speak up when needed.

That meant that if I saw someone on my team do or say something that wasn't the right thing to do, I would stop them and explain that we don't do things that way. Then I'd tell them how it should be done and why. The goal wasn't to humiliate or penalize anyone, but to educate them, to spread the Cintas principal objective far and wide, and to help everyone row in the same direction.

I remember when I had a new employee—a group vice president—who, shortly after being hired, went on a trip visiting our plants. While he was out, I discovered that I needed to discuss something with him, so I called his administrative assistant to try to track him down (this was before the ubiquity of cell phones). She told me that he was at our plant in Philadelphia that day, so I called the Philadelphia plant. To my surprise, they told me he wasn't there. Not only that, but they had no idea he was supposed to be there; they weren't expecting him.

When the group vice president returned to the office on Monday, I sat him down for a chat. I explained, "When you say you're going to Philadelphia, you'd better be going to Philadelphia. You told your administrative assistant you were going to be there, but we both know you weren't. I don't know where you actually were, but if I ever ask your administrative assistant where you are and you turn out not to be where you say you are, you won't be working here anymore. Is that understood?"

The issue for me, mainly, was that he wasn't where he said he was going to be. Doing what you promise you'll do is part of living up to your commitments and doing your best work for our customers. It all ties back to the principal objective.

WHAT HAPPENS TO COMPANIES WITHOUT A PRINCIPAL OBJECTIVE?

Just as a principal objective makes decision-making easier, the lack of a principal objective leads decisions to be driven by other factors, such as ego, greed, and the benefit of those at the top of the hierarchy. Without a principal objective, decisions are driven by what is best for a subset of the constituents—not the employees, not the shareholders, not the customers, but the two, three, or four people at the top.

That's not what should drive decisions, nor is that a sustainable strategy for success.

Finding a way to make employees the source of your competitive advantage is what will drive customer satisfaction and profits within any organization. And your principal objective should reflect how you will make that happen.

CHAPTER SUMMARY

- Commit to writing what you believe your organization's principal objective should be.
- Communicate that principal objective ad nauseum, and then do it some more.
- Constantly reinforce that objective within your organization and introduce it to new hires. Be sure it's understood and being applied consistently within your organization.
- Use it as a tool to evaluate the compatibility of potential new hires, confirming that the principal objective is clear and is aligned with how candidates live and work.

CHAPTER 2

DEFINING YOUR CORPORATE CHARACTER

The first component of the Cintas culture was its principal objective. The second was its corporate character, which represented the company's values and philosophy about how, as an organization, it should operate. Character, for us, reflected everything from how we acted toward our customers and toward each other to how we dressed; how we carried ourselves; what our facilities looked like; and what our communications, including memos, proposals, letters, and emails, looked and sounded like. In all cases, professionalism was the hallmark. It was the one quality we wanted Cintas to be known for above all else.

However, corporate character wasn't an idea senior management sprung on all of our partners out of the blue one day. It was already evident at Cintas when we turned our attention to defining and communicating it. The Cintas corporate culture became increasingly important as the company's growth rate picked up. With new working partners regularly joining the team, we knew we needed to define the company's character so that we could convey expectations company-wide, to our partners old and new. Only then could we hope to standardize how things were done at Cintas.

By the same token, being able to clearly articulate our corporate character also made it easier to recognize language and behavior that were inconsistent with the desired Cintas reputation. When our corporate character was crystal clear, then when someone did something that was completely out of character, or out of sync with set expectations, it was easy to spot. The sooner bad behavior was addressed, the easier it was to rectify or change.

Of course, it was much easier to train or socialize a newer partner who had just graduated from college, as was the case with many of our management trainees. Today, I would guess, 80 to 90 percent of the people running Cintas actually started as management trainees. Being able to teach a new partner "the Cintas way" was easier when they hadn't already learned the Procter & Gamble way, or the IBM way, first. That's not to say we didn't hire from the outside when we needed a particular skill set or experience—we did—but when we did, the odds were also good that hire would need to be retrained or need to adjust their behavior and mannerisms to match Cintas's. That's how they became one of us.

Where online shoe retailer Zappos is known far and wide for its commitment to customer service, often sending out multiple sizes of a pair of shoes in one shipment to ensure that a customer finds the right size; and L.L. Bean is known for the durability of its gear and its generous return policy; and Tesla is known for innovation, thanks to its industry leadership in developing electric vehicles, Cintas wanted to be known for its professionalism.

IN THE IMAGE BUSINESS

Professionalism was the first word that came to mind when we at Cintas thought about our corporate character. Much like how our principle objective made clear the importance of taking care of our partners, in order to do the best job possible for our customers and shareholders, the concept of professionalism drove our corporate character.

Being in the image business was the major reason we looked for ways to convey our professionalism. That meant that everyone in the company was expected to wear business suits; that hasn't changed. We've never gone to corporate casual dress. Even today, partners are expected to wear suits, dress shirts, and ties (for men) every day to work. We made that conscious decision for two reasons: (1) we didn't think khakis and a polo shirt looked as professional as did wearing a suit and (2) if we were trying to convince our customers how important it was to have a corporate uniform, we'd better have had one ourselves.

Cintas sells professional-looking uniforms to airlines, to hotels, to everywhere from the corner gas station to the Four Seasons Hotel, so we felt that, as a company, we should have our own uniform. And we do.

A professional appearance carried over to other aspects of our business, too, such as our facilities. Although they weren't fancy or opulent—some might even say they were spartan—our plants and offices were attractive and extremely clean. We were so committed to cleanliness that you could eat off the floor in our plants—even in the industrial laundry, where uniforms and towels caked with soil, grease, and oil came in for cleaning.

Walking into one of our plants felt like you were walking into a hospital; they were so tidy and sterile looking. Because so much heat was generated by the equipment in what we referred to as the washroom— where incoming uniforms were washed and we air-conditioned all of our plants to make the temperature comfortable for our partners. We painted the floors, and we regularly repainted them to ensure that they looked clean and new. We provided space for tools and materials to be neatly stored. And at the end of each shift, workers were given 10 or 15 minutes to clean up their work area so that they could leave it the way they found it at the start of their shift.

Cleanliness extended to our trucks as well. At last count, I believe Cintas had the sixth-largest fleet of trucks in the US. And we understood what an important marketing tool those delivery trucks were. A study I read years ago reported that in a city of one million, one truck made one million impressions a year. Those trucks are seen out and about when people are driving alongside them on the highway, when they are parked in a parking lot and making a delivery, and when they are on a street returning to the plant. They are one of our most visible marketing machines, really, which is why we decided that they needed to be pristine at all times. We called it the UPS standard, because you never see a dirty UPS truck; they just wouldn't let it go out with road dust and grime.

So we, too, became very focused on the appearance of our vehicles. They needed to be sparkling clean inside and out any time they were not parked at our facilities. They represented Cintas every time they left, so just as our partners were expected to wear business suits to work, our trucks were expected to be clean and in good repair at all times. After all, what kind of image would we portray as a cleaning business if we were comfortable sending out trucks that were dirty, rusty, and beat up?

I remember one time I had to make that very case to the general manager of our Columbus, Ohio, plant years ago. I was on-site for some meetings, and at the end of the day, I walked to the back where the trucks were parked. Many of them were very dirty, so I called the general manager over to talk to him about it.

"Jay," I said, "look at these trucks. They're dirty, but we don't have dirty trucks. What's going on?"

"Well, we've had a lot of rain recently, so I've been washing the trucks twice a week," he told me. "Maybe I need to do it more often. How many times a week do you think I should be washing them?" he asked me.

"As many times as you have to in order to be sure they are always clean and in good repair," I responded. "I don't care if you have to wash them four times a day if that's what it will take to make them free of dirt and dust."

He got the point. The trucks were washed regularly from then on.

Another time, I was driving to work one morning, and I happened to get behind one of our trucks. It was a very cold that morning, I remember, and the truck had not been properly washed, it appeared. It was very dirty. So from my car, I called the general manager to ask about truck 3247.

"Jim, I'm driving behind truck 3247, and it's first thing in the morning, and it's not clean. What's going on?"

"Bob," he said, "we had a problem with our washing system last night because it got so cold and the water froze, so we couldn't wash all of our trucks."

"What's our policy with our trucks?" I asked him.

"That they need to be clean and in good repair in order to be out on the road," Jim replied.

"Was there any exception to that rule, such as for water freezing?" I asked.

"No," he said. "I got it."

We were fanatics about cleanliness and image. We understood that everything we did required Cintas partners to look, act, and behave like pros at all times, in order to be recognized as the professionals that we were. That was the essence of our corporate character.

THE SAFEKEEPING OF OUR PARTNERS

Safety was a core component too. We really got focused on providing a safe workplace for our partners about 20 years ago, in the early 2000s. We had a terrible accident that occurred in one of our plants that really caused us to increase our attention to safety. We always had a good safety record, but this accident motivated us to redouble our efforts on safety.

That tragedy pushed Cintas to improve its whole approach to safety. We wanted our people to go home to their families every night the same way they came to work in the morning. We never wanted an accident like that to happen again, so we spent a lot of time on a regular basis asking how we could make a process or a piece of equipment safer to use.

One step we took was to have Safety and Improvement Committee meetings every month, in every plant. Those meetings were to hear from partners who worked in the plants every day what the company could do both to make it a safer workplace and to make it a better place to work—a place they were proud to work for.

Not everyone was invited to those monthly meetings at once, however. To give partners plenty of time to express themselves and be heard, of the 200 or so plant employees, a handful of randomly selected people would come together to brainstorm ways Cintas could improve safety. There would be a mix of service salespeople (truck drivers), administrative professionals, and production partners who would sit down with the general manager for a couple of hours to discuss what was going well in the plant, what was frustrating, and whether there were any safety issues that someone had spotted that needed to be addressed. The group would chat about whether vehicles were in good condition, what customers were saying, what people were concerned about, and where there were opportunities for improvement. The general manager took notes and then typed them up and sent them to their boss. At the start of each meeting, the committee would get a rundown of all the points made at the last meeting and hear what the general manager had done so far to address them in the last month. That was important, so that committee members understood that their voices mattered and that their roles were important.

Each individual selected served a year-long term and was then replaced by someone new, to continue to get new perspectives from different departments and groups within each plant. Involving partners from a broad cross section of the company was designed to drive home the point that everyone was responsible for safety. Everyone had an important role to play.

FEELING COMFORTABLE ENOUGH TO SPEAK UP

Although Cintas people worked hard to present a professional image to the outside world, inside, the professional relationships were close and collegial. Yes, there was an organizational hierarchy, but partners at all levels were encouraged to interact with each other and with management. We felt it was critical to create an environment where it was perfectly acceptable to talk to the boss or the boss's boss. We wanted partners to know that management wanted to know what they thought or what they might recommend. Because the people on the front line are closer to the problem than any manager or CEO would be, the partners were in a much better position to recognize issues and propose solutions to them. It was important, however, for the boss who was approached with a new idea or an observation to act on it. If partners were encouraged to speak up but then never heard another word about their idea or didn't see that an issue they brought up was addressed, they wouldn't bother to approach their boss in the future. They needed to feel comfortable speaking up and confident that what they shared would be a catalyst for positive change. They could make a difference.

We had an open-door policy that encouraged partners to stop by and speak up when they felt called to. The vast majority of partners knew the top person in their location, whether it was a plant general manager or a business unit president. In fact, they typically knew that person very well and felt confident that if they stopped to talk to them, that supervisor or manager would be very happy to listen to whatever they had to say.

Those personal connections were part of our culture, and they were good for the company as a whole and helped it perform at a very high level. Senior leaders were then very well informed or plugged in to what was going on, because partners felt comfortable speaking up about some-one whom they felt wasn't a good fit for Cintas or about a customer situation that wasn't being addressed, for example.

Partners who knew their input was valued and welcome had no qualms about stopping by the CEO's or general manager's office to express concern about a new supervisor or a new manager. Partners understood that it was up to them to say something if there was a problem; that was the only way the company could improve. At Cintas, partners spoke up regularly. By the same token, senior leaders and managers also went out onto the plant floor to talk to partners regularly. They didn't just sit in their offices and wait for partners to come to them; they made an effort to be available if people had questions or wanted to point something out. When I was CEO, I tried to sit down and have lunch with partners on a regular basis—office clerks, production partners, you name it—so that we could chat casually about how things were going, what we could do to make their work go smoother, or whether there was any issue that was bugging them. Striking up those casual conversations really helped prevent surprises.

One tool we used to encourage internal communication was our hotline, which used to be a written letter but now is an actual phone line where messages can be left. When partners wanted me to know about something but hadn't had a chance to chat in person, they'd write up a hotline message and send it to me. The hotline turned out to be useful for providing feedback on new hires, especially.

I remember one year we had transferred someone in to become the new manager in one of our distribution centers. And as soon as that individual assumed that role, I started getting hotline messages. All told, I received six different messages from six different people, all saying essentially the same thing: "You made a mistake."

One of the letters provided helpful detail about the situation that I'm not sure I would have recognized otherwise. The letter said:

> We don't have anything against the new manager you brought in, but you picked the wrong person. Mary, who works here, is a superstar. We all love her. She works her tail off, she knows the business inside and out, and she loves Cintas. I don't understand why you didn't consider her for this position?!

Honestly, I don't think we considered Mary for the position because we had someone else already trained who wanted to be transferred. But after reading so many hotlines, I decided I needed to go meet with the six partners to talk.

I headed to the location and sat down with the partners to understand more clearly why Mary was a better fit for the job than the person we had brought in. It turns out we had completely overlooked the possibility of promoting Mary when she was truly the perfect choice. We had made a mistake, and I made sure we corrected it immediately. We promoted Mary into the manager role and transferred the other supervisor back to their old location. That partner hadn't done anything wrong, but we had made an error in not promoting from within the plant, especially when there was a high performer ready for a new challenge.

But I never would have known about that whole situation without setting up a system to collect feedback from our partners.

That's not to say that all hotline messages were about other people, however. Sometimes partners would submit concerns about their own jobs, like Susan did a few years back. My team and I looked into each and every message we received, so when I saw that Susan wrote that she was scared she was going to lose her job, I wanted to understand what was going on.

In her letter, she told me, "I need my job. I did miss a little bit of work, but I've been told that if I come in late one more time, I'm going to be fired." This sounded pretty harsh and more than a little suspicious to me, because we didn't fire people for being occasionally late, especially if there were extenuating circumstances. So I called to learn more about what was going on.

"Susan, I understand you're worried about losing your job. How long have you worked for us?" I asked her.

"Seven months," she replied.

"And how many times have you been late?" I asked.

"Well, I'm usually late a couple times a week," she admitted.

"How much time have you missed?" I wondered.

"I've missed three or four days a month," she told me. (Doing the math in my head, I knew that was nearly a month of work in just the seven months she'd been on payroll.)

"Why are you missing so much time?" I asked her.

"I have a young child, and sometimes my babysitter doesn't show up on time," she explained. "I have an old car, and sometimes it doesn't start." She continued with a few more reasons for her inconsistent performance.

Knowing that typically what someone admits to is not quite the whole truth—I've found it's usually about 50 percent worse than they're letting on—I had to be honest with her.

"Susan, I probably would have fired you four or five months ago," I told her. "I'm a parent, so I understand that children have to come first. And I understand that your car may not function properly, and that's tough. But what you need to understand is that when you don't come to work, or you come in late, everyone else has to pick up the slack—to effectively fill in for you. You're putting a tremendous burden not just on the company but also on your boss and your coworkers. Not only is that unfair to them but also we have a company that's very efficient. We have exactly as many people as we need to do the work, so when you don't come in and you're in a department of six people, the other five people have to do their jobs and yours.

"So if you can't figure out how to solve your childcare and transportation issues, then you probably need to work someplace else—someplace where it's not a big deal if you're late or you miss a few days of work each month," I told her. She did admit that she was to blame for the situation, and I offered some suggestions for solving her problems, but I didn't give her the sympathy she was after.

Although Susan probably didn't get the answer she was looking for, the hotline program was a success because partners knew that if they submitted a letter, it was going to trigger an investigation at some level. Whether a supervisor was treating people poorly, or partners were doing things they shouldn't be, or there was an issue in a particular department, we would hear about it. And everyone knew that action would be taken—hotline messages weren't ignored.

THE CUSTOMER IS ALWAYS RIGHT

Many companies talk about their focus on their customer, but that's not actually the case. Their focus isn't really on customer satisfaction, as you've no doubt experienced recently if you've eaten a dinner out or spent time shopping in a store. Sometimes customers are made to feel like nuisances.

At Cintas, we worked hard to do the exact opposite. We wanted our customers to feel revered, because they were. If it weren't for our customers, no Cintas partners would get paychecks, we wouldn't be able to buy uniforms or trucks, and we certainly wouldn't be able to expand and open new plants or offices. Customers were what made all of that possible. All of the revenue that Cintas generated was from one source: customers. So in order to stay in business, we needed to make sure our customers were happy.

That's true whether you're dealing with a dream of a customer who is happy with everything you do or the customer who is rude and disrespectful. All customers should be treated with reverence.

That said, when we did encounter a customer who was impossible to satisfy, we didn't quit and tell them, "You're a jerk, and we don't want to do business with you anymore." Instead, we took the blame. "We've failed you," we'd say. "We have tried everything we know to make you happy and earn your respect, and we just haven't been successful in doing that. So we're going to help you find a new supplier. We're so disappointed that we couldn't give you what you needed, but we assure you that we'll find a different supplier."

Sometimes, that conversation turned the relationship around for the better. In many cases, the customer was unaware how they had been coming across and would respond with, "What are you talking about? We're very satisfied."

In other cases, we would connect them with a competitor, and then, three or four months later, they would often come back to us and want to reestablish the relationship because they realized that the quality of service we had been providing was superior to anything else on the market.

But our ability to satisfy our customers depended almost entirely on our frontline workers: the people who were regularly face-to-face with our customers or doing the behind-the-scenes work to provide the products and services they expected.

RESPECT FOR EACH WORKER

It's easy to lose sight of the fact that managers and senior executives are really nothing more than overhead. They're not the partners doing the work that generates revenue for the company. The people making money for Cintas were operating the washing machines and driving the trucks and answering questions from customers by phone. They were the rainmakers, truly. And managers like me were nothing more than overhead.

My son, Brent, drove that home for me years ago when, at age 10, he asked me what I did at Cintas. At the time I was executive vice president and was responsible for acquisitions and long-range planning. To a 10-year-old, that didn't mean much, I quickly learned. I tried several different ways to explain my role without success. Then he asked me,

"Do you drive a truck?" "No," I told him. "Do you clean the uniforms?" "No," I told him again. "Do you sell the uniforms?" he wanted to know. "No," I had to admit. That's the exact moment it dawned on me that I wasn't adding much value at all by comparison to the people on the front line.

Perhaps that's why respect for our partners is required within Cintas. They're the ones doing the hard work, and management is well aware of this fact.

Courtesy was another important character of Cintas partners; it was part of the corporate character. Being respectful to everyone, even a belligerent customer, was important to us. We expected everyone in the company to treat each other the same way they'd treat a brother or sister or their mother or father. "If you treat them that way, you're more likely to develop the kind of relationship with them that you want to have," I'd tell our partners. Treat your colleagues and coworkers as you would treat a dear family member and they're likely to become someone you are close to.

Of course, things weren't always perfect. Sometimes tough conversations were required to get things back on track. That was another tenet of the Cintas corporate character: directness. It was rarely easy to deliver constructive criticism or negative feedback, but when in the interest of the company, tough conversations had to occur.

One of the benefits of keeping lines of communication open and dealing with difficult situations head-on and quickly was that there wasn't much opportunity for complaining. We looked to hire partners who were enthusiastic about whatever they were doing. We wanted positivity as part of our culture, so we hired for it. We looked for a positive attitude and a willingness to learn. Partners with those characteristics were much less likely to blame others or to whine and complain yet more likely to approach situations with a solutions mindset. Enthusiasm was big for us.

Another characteristic that was essential for success at Cintas was moral and ethical standards. We looked for people who were "straight arrows," so to speak. We tried to steer clear of people who were likely to engage in any form of discrimination or sexual harassment or unethical dealings. I think most people know in their gut what is right and what is wrong, and we looked for people who had the discipline to say no to opportunities that would lead to unethical behavior or choices that would reflect poorly on Cintas.

COMPETITIVE URGENCY

You've probably heard the phrase "sense of urgency," which refers to a willingness to move quickly when action is required. At Cintas, we took that notion a step further, to the concept of competitive urgency. We defined competitive urgency as attending to every detail as if the satisfaction of that detail would make the difference between satisfying or saving a customer and not or between satisfying or saving a partner and not.

Too often, people get bogged down in the daily minutiae, such as email messages, meetings, reading reports, etc., that generally have no material impact on customers or partners or shareholders, the three components of our principal objective. We expected that when our partners saw a problem with a customer, they would fix it—now. When they saw a problem with a partner, they fixed it—now. And if the problem couldn't be fixed on the spot, they would make a commitment to that customer or partner to get back to them with an answer or a solution, say, by Friday. Then they would get back with an answer or solution by Friday. Because if Cintas took care of those two groups—customers and partners—everything else would be fine.

We were constantly raising the bar on our own performance, expecting more of ourselves in the pursuit of meeting or exceeding customer expectations. Dick referred to it as "positive discontent," a term I believe Peter Drucker originated.

Positive discontent is the belief that anything can be done better. By investing effort in improving every product, every service, every plant, every truck—everything we were doing—we could earn and maintain a competitive advantage. But we needed continuous improvement in order to hold that position.

We were never satisfied, and that's a good thing. We were optimistic that we could always be better, and so, as a company, we constantly strived for improvement.

CHAPTER SUMMARY

- Corporate character is the word or image that comes to mind when you talk about a company. At Cintas, our word was "professionalism."
- Encourage and invite communication from employees at all levels of the company. Set up tools to make it easy for them to share ideas, suggestions, and feedback with you.
- Revering your customer and committing your company to serving them to the best of your ability will lead to success. Customers who can't be satisfied shouldn't be blamed but rather referred to a competitor who may have better luck meeting their needs.
- At Cintas, we were aware that we could always improve and we could always do something better, which is the concept of positive discontent. The day we are satisfied is the day we will stop getting better. By looking for opportunities for continuous improvement, we could achieve a leadership position and stay there, ahead of our competition.

CHAPTER 3

ESTABLISHING MANAGEMENT SYSTEMS

Early on, as Cintas grew, Dick became increasingly concerned with consistency across the organization. Within the small company, partners were often promoted fairly quickly into supervisory roles, where they were responsible for overseeing others' work. Dick's main focus at that time was helping the company grow, but he began to notice more discrepancies between how he would have handled a situation and how the new supervisors were dealing with things. He felt like he was losing control and partners were deciding for themselves how to handle situations, rather than following the directions he had given them.

The problem was a lack of consistency. Dick had tried to convey exactly how he expected processes to run on an individual basis, but that was problematic or, apparently, ineffective.

As partners were promoted, Dick would sit down with them individually to explain how he wanted things done. He would say, "When this happens, here's how you handle it," or "When that happens, do that." To him, it was very clear how things should run. However, new supervisors may have heard his instructions a little differently from how he intended, or they interpreted his instructions in a slightly different way, so when they would run into one of the situations Dick had described, they would take an approach that varied from what he expected. The result was differing tactics company-wide.

Although Dick recognized the problem, he wasn't sure at first how to address it, how to bring everyone into alignment.

Then he came across a book by McKinsey & Company consultant Marvin Brower, titled *The Will to Manage: Corporate Success through Programmed Management*, which advocated the need to set objectives and document internal business processes.

Brower's definition of management would help to define Cintas's own management process for years to come. His definition was:

> *Managing is the activity or task of determining the objectives of an organization and then guiding the people and other resources of the organization in the successful achievement of those objectives.*

By documenting who, exactly, was permitted to approve budget items over a certain amount, or what the process was for buying a new truck, Brower said, you could create an operations manual that would promote consistency of process.

In fact, *The Will to Manage* laid out 14 processes "from which a management system for any business can be fashioned," Brower said. And Dick studied each and every one of them. They were:

1. Setting objectives—"Deciding on the business in which the company should engage."
2. Planning strategy—"Developing concepts, ideas, and plans for achieving objectives successfully."
3. Establishing goals—Setting shorter-term goals, then larger objectives.
4. Developing a company philosophy—Establishing the beliefs, values, attitudes, and guidelines that make up "the way we do things around here."
5. Establishing policies—Plans for action to carry out strategies.
6. Planning the organizational structure—Pulling people together in performing activities.

7. Providing personnel—Recruiting, selecting, and developing people.
8. Establishing procedures—How activities should be carried out.
9. Providing facilities—Procuring property, plant, and equipment necessary to operate the business.
10. Providing capital—Obtaining funds needed to operate and grow the venture.
11. Setting standards—"Establishing measures of performance to help the company achieve its objective."
12. Providing control information—Supplying facts and figures for effective decision-making.
13. Activating people—"Commanding and motivating people to act in accordance with philosophies, policies, and procedures in carrying out company plans."

Dick became a devotee of Brower's process and immediately began work to document solutions to recurring questions or problems. Over time, the Cintas operations manual had answers to virtually any question a partner might have. What's the appropriate way to answer the phone? How should customer proposals be formatted and presented? Not sure what to do when there's an accident in your plant? The instructions were clearly laid out in the manual. Over time, one by one, recurring processes were documented and added to the manual.

The Cintas operations manual was the first thing I was handed when I joined the company. Dick told me to read it because "this is the way we run the company," he explained.

In addition to improving consistency across processes, documenting processes also became a great training tool. Rather than having new employees learn on their own what works and what doesn't, by writing down scenarios as they came up and providing the Cintas solution or approach, new partners could save time and energy by simply referring to the manual for how they should respond. If their particular question wasn't addressed in the manual, we saw it as an opportunity to add new information.

People who hadn't faced certain business situations before also had the benefit of access to experienced partners who had been working at Cintas longer than they had. Whenever I encountered a problem I didn't know how to address or had a difficult decision to make, I made a habit of turning to people I respected who I thought likely had faced a similar situation in their past. I'd ask for their input and guidance regarding how they had tackled a similar situation in their career or how they would likely resolve it, given what they knew from their own work life. Of course, taking the time to approach an expert to get their feedback was time-consuming and not necessarily efficient, though it was certainly effective.

The Cintas operations manual was the company's attempt to compile the experiences and expertise of its most skilled managers, so that when a question arose about how to handle a situation, partners didn't have to hunt down a supervisor or manager; they could open the manual and read the company's policy and procedure. That manual was the culmination of the knowledge and experience of all the people in the company who had previously encountered the same problem. It was a written record of that wisdom that was accessible by anyone in Cintas's employ.

With such specific guidelines regarding how decisions were to be made and who had the authority to make them, there were fewer opportunities for individuals to go off-script, as it were—meaning there were fewer chances for partners to take matters into their own hands and make decisions that weren't guided by the manual.

Without guidelines, there is no managerial control within an organization. Although management may believe they have clearly laid out instructions for how work is to be done, unless it is committed to writing and communicated, it is very likely that different teams or business units or facilities operate very differently from one another. I saw it quite a bit as I visited with Cintas customers. I would visit one customer's plant and then visit another, only to find that it operated completely differently. Managers there were given the leeway, maybe unbeknownst to senior leadership, to make decisions themselves for how work was to be done. The person running each plant dictated the policies and procedures according to their own experiences and beliefs or interpretations of their company's policies, rather than following detailed instructions from headquarters about how situations were to be dealt with across the company.

THE DANGER OF INTERPRETATION

I witnessed this situation firsthand in 1980 while Cintas was doing its due diligence on a company in Houston that we were considering buying. I was responsible for assessing whether the company would fit with the Cintas culture, among other things. I started at the company's largest plant and met with the general manager there, Dave Hoyt. At one point I asked him, "Dave, do you have bonus programs here at your company?"

"Yes," he responded.

"How many people are entitled to potential bonuses?" I asked.

"Well, about eight or nine. Seven or eight of my direct reports and I have bonus programs to incentivize good performance," he told me.

"That's great," I told him, glad to be aware of such an agreement.

I proceeded to visit the six other plants the company owned and heard the same story. In each plant, the general manager and his or her direct reports all had bonuses in place to reward top performance.

Another important question I had for the general managers had to do with customer contracts. I asked each one a variation of "Do you have contracts with all of your customers?"

And at each one I heard reasons why they did not have contracts with some of their customers, ranging from having had a bad experience with another vendor thanks to a contract, to being concerned about what could go wrong in the future if they were contractually bound.

"So you went ahead and did business with them anyway?" I asked.

"Yes," I heard from each manager.

This was concerning to me because of Cintas's need to make a significant upfront investment in the products we would then rent to our customers. We asked our customers to sign a contract so that we could at least be assured that our costs would be covered if, for example, two weeks after signing it, the company suddenly decided uniforms weren't for them. Without a contract, we were at risk of losing the thousands of dollars we had just spent having custom uniforms designed and produced.

After touring all of the plants, Dick and I went back to meet with the company's owner, Bill Hawkins. Bill was a wonderful man, extremely honorable, and we were delighted to potentially be doing business with him. But what I had learned from his general managers didn't match what he had told us at the beginning of our negotiations and on which our purchase offer was based.

Bill had told us quite confidently that "the general managers are the only employees with bonus programs" and "we have contracts with all of our customers; we will not do business with a customer without a contract in place." Yet, in fact, he was mistaken.

Shocked, he immediately picked up the phone and dialed Dave Hoyt for confirmation.

"Dave, I'm sitting here with Bob Kohlhepp, and he tells me you have eight bonus programs just in Houston. Is that right?" Bill asked.

"Yes, sir, it is," Dave told him.

Perplexed, Bill told him, "Dave, I don't understand why you did that. I never told you it was OK to have eight bonus programs!"

"Well, you never told me it wasn't OK," was Dave's response. "I thought my bonus program worked well for me, so I gave it to the eight people who report directly to me," he explained.

No one had ever told him he couldn't set up a bonus program, so he did. And that's at the core of what happens when there is no system in place. Without clear guidelines, employees may assume that they have the latitude and the authority to do what they think is in the company's best interest, like offering bonuses to other employees and making contracts optional. This lack of understanding regarding procedures and authority created serious problems, not the least of which was devaluing the company as a whole.

That approach of asking frontline workers about their responsibilities was one way we were able to identify disconnects between stated processes and actual processes. We always started at the lowest level. For example, we had a 10-week training program for all new service sales representatives, but if I wanted to verify that everyone was being put through that full 10-week course, I asked the partners—not the managers. And if I heard anything other than 10 weeks as the length of their training, there was a problem.

The way you find out how a company is managed is by talking to employees, not managers. Management will always tell you how it's supposed to be or the way they think things are running. But when you talk to the people on the front line, you find out the way it really is. And in many cases, the two answers are quite different. If you don't have a system in place, it happens all the time.

At Cintas, the operations manual laid out in great detail who was authorized to have a bonus program, what the bonus program entailed, and what it was supposed to look like. The problem at Bill Hawkins's company was that he, the owner, thought things were being run one way, but, in fact, his direct reports had made decisions about how they thought things should work that differed from Bill's vision. The company was being run substantially differently from what was expected because of a lack of documented systems.

CREATING A DYNAMIC MANAGEMENT SYSTEM

Although management systems need to be clear-cut, they also need to be adjustable, to be modified or revised as the environment in which you're working changes. You create policies and procedures based on current conditions, but you should also be aware that those conditions will eventually change, because of either external forces or internal ones.

Cintas learned that lesson early on, when it was a very small company with a small number of employees. We caught a partner stealing and knew we had to let him go. Not only could we not trust him if he was stealing but also we had mandated in our operations manual that stealing was cause for immediate termination. We fired him.

We quickly found out, however, that we didn't just lose one employee—we lost four. The fired employee's two brothers and nephew were also on our payroll and promptly quit when he was let go. Together they represented about 30 percent of our workforce in that one plant of around 13 partners. It was a major blow that we hadn't anticipated, and we needed to change our policies and procedures to prevent it from happening again.

What that meant was that immediate family members of current partners could not be hired. For many years, that was the strict rule.

Then, as the company grew, management decided it would be smart to reevaluate that policy. It had served Cintas well for quite a while, but when a new uniform manufacturing plant was being established in a rural community in Kentucky, we discovered it was too restrictive. The general manager needed 150 workers total. He successfully hired 80 but then found it nearly impossible to hire more because all the other candidates were related to someone else who had just been hired.

He told me, "Bob, I can't staff this plant with that policy in place."

So we changed it. Today the policy is that family members of current partners *can* be hired, but they can't directly report to their relative. The only exception is officers; family members of officers cannot not be hired, with few exceptions.

Exceptions were rare but did occur from time to time, reflecting the need for policies to adapt to changing conditions. Policies were set with the understanding that they wouldn't apply to every single situation that arises. Therefore, as a manager at Cintas, you not only had the right but also the responsibility to request an exception when you believed the application of a policy was not in the company's best interest. We didn't want people to follow a policy to the letter of the law if it resulted in a poor outcome for the company. We wanted them to simply make a case for an exception—providing a reason that the policy should be waived in that situation.

We also told our partners that if they were faced with a situation where, in their judgment, implementing a policy was not the best decision and they did not have time to request an exception, they should use their best judgment and tell their boss about it after the fact.

Of course, there was a procedure for making an exception that you needed to follow, and we kept close track of all the exceptions. If we saw that a particular policy required frequent exceptions, we knew it was likely a policy that was no longer appropriate and should be changed. We certainly didn't want partners following policies without question, because in some cases those policies were outdated and needed to be revised.

Cintas actually has a policy committee of approximately 20 people who serve for a year and who are responsible for reviewing requests to change policies. The process involves writing a cover memo explaining why the partner feels that a policy should be changed and attaching a proposed revised policy. The committee then considers requests for policy changes, and a final decision is made by the CEO.

On an annual basis, we might change 10 or so policies of the 50 or 60 reviewed per year. Sometimes policies were changed because a law changed or something else externally forced it. Other times, as a company, Cintas might decide to modify a policy, such as changing the time required before being vested in the retirement plan from seven years to five; or if the health insurance policy changed and introduced a new lifetime cap on claims, Cintas would update its policies to reflect that.

Additionally, a policy created decades ago, when the organization was only a few dozen people, is unlikely to still be relevant—or at least as effective—when the company is now hundreds or thousands of people strong. In many situations, old policies need to be updated because they no longer apply as they were originally written.

To ensure that management policies were relevant, Cintas would review each and every one annually. The management team would ask, "Do we still need this policy?" Someone would be assigned responsibility for carefully investigating the ramifications of that policy and then recommending whether it needed to be updated or whether it was current and effective as is. We wanted to avoid having rules in place that were no longer useful.

A perfect example of having outdated policies is the US Social Security retirement age. When the qualification age for Social Security was set at 65 many decades ago, the average life expectancy was likely in the 60s or 70s. Today, many people live into their 80s and 90s, so is age 65 a good representation of when people should be expected to retire? Probably not, but the government won't consider modifying it because of the political ramifications.

So what happens is that bureaucracy is introduced that is unnecessary and often irrelevant, which can impede progress. At Cintas, we wanted to avoid that.

CONSISTENCY IS KING

The goal of introducing policies and procedures to get everyone working in sync is consistency. Assuring customers that they can expect the same level of service, the same quality of garment, the same professionalism at every level of the company is what consistency looks like. McDonald's is the quintessential example of consistency, in my mind.

Ray Kroc, who bought and expanded McDonald's, understood how critical sameness was throughout his growing chain of restaurants. He promised customers that a Big Mac purchased in Cincinnati would look and taste exactly the same as a Big Mac purchased in New York City, Miami, Dallas, or Seattle. To make that promise, he developed very specific instructions regarding how every Big Mac should be made, from how the buns are baked to where the beef is purchased, how long it cooks on the grill, how many ounces of lettuce should be placed on each patty and where, and so on. The same is true for every other process throughout the restaurant. There are detailed instructions for how food is prepared, how the soda machines are cleaned, how the cash registers are emptied each night, how the floors are mopped, and how employees are hired and fired, to name just a few procedures.

Ray Kroc wanted to be absolutely sure that if you drove through a McDonald's drive-through and ordered a Big Mac, you would know exactly what it was going to taste like, no matter where in the world you were.

Procter & Gamble, another leading company, does the same thing. Relentless documentation of processes made consistency possible throughout the organization.

Great companies have operational systems. However, those systems aren't static. They have to be kept up-to-date, they have to be appropriate for the environment that your company is currently operating in, and they need to be written such that everyone understands that exceptions are OK, as long as the process to request an exception is followed.

CULTURE AS COMPETITIVE ADVANTAGE

Cintas certainly modeled some of its processes and procedures after other market leaders, just as other companies routinely copied us. We were never concerned about other companies copying us, however, because Cintas was always striving for continuous improvement. By the time a competitor caught wind of a new approach we had taken, a strategy we had adopted, or a new policy we had introduced, we were already five more steps ahead of them.

Sure, other companies could copy our procedures, but they couldn't replicate the corporate culture we had carefully cultivated over many years. It's nearly impossible to emulate a culture, because it's intangible. You can't see it. You can't feel it. And it's based on the many personalities, experiences, and understandings of the employees, which no other organization could match exactly.

The same situation occurred years ago, in the 1970s and 1980s, when Japanese car makers were winning market share from American car companies without even trying. So executives from General Motors and Ford would tour Japanese companies to try to identify what they were doing that made them so successful. And those same executives would come back and report, "Well, their plants look exactly like our plants, and they seem to operate the same way we operate."

Yes, the equipment and the materials and even the processes could be the same, and yet the companies were vastly different, all because of culture.

What the Americans didn't see was the Japanese system of kaizen—of continuous improvement—where frontline workers were encouraged to point out ways to improve even the most minute part of a process. They were encouraged to look for ways to complete tasks faster or better or with less effort, for example; and with an entire organization on the hunt for ways to make a process better, it was in a constant state of improvement. That aspect of the company was behind-the-scenes, and the Americans failed to spot it.

That continuous improvement focus was the ultimate competitive advantage for the Japanese, just as the Cintas culture of professionalism was our insurmountable advantage.

For a culture to remain an advantage, however, it needs to be enduring. It needs to survive the transition to new leadership. This all means that it can't be based on a particular CEO's personality or following. Culture has to permeate the entire organization, so that when a CEO leaves or retires, the company keeps right on humming just as before.

For a lesson in what can happen when culture is *not* instilled throughout an organization, you need only look at Chrysler and Lee Iacocca.

When Lee Iacocca took over as CEO at Chrysler in 1978, the Detroit automaker was hemorrhaging cash and on the verge of going under. Recalls of the Dodge and Plymouth Volare had cost Chrysler billions, and within his first year at the helm, Iacocca had to turn to the US government to request a $1.5-billion bailout, in the form of loan guarantees, in order to stay in business. He also took the symbolic step of cutting his salary to $1.

That got the public's attention, sparking a shift in attitude toward Chrysler that brought out support across the board for him and for the company. Everyone, from celebrities to local politicians to union bosses, was suddenly rooting for Chrysler's success.

Iacocca also put himself on the front line by appearing in Chrysler's commercials, reassuring America and Chrysler workers that "the pride is back." As pride of workmanship returned, that message shifted to "If you can find a better car, buy it."

Iacocca had effectively installed himself as Chrysler's figurehead.

Behind the scenes, he was hard at work, too, however. He quickly fired 33 of the company's 35 vice presidents and brought in his own, albeit leaner, team. He righted the auto design process, starting with asking dealers what buyers wanted, rather than throwing cars together in the hopes that drivers would buy; this helped earn back the trust of its dealer network. And he directed attention to improving the company's poor production reputation.

The results were almost immediate.

Chrysler released the first of its bestselling K-car line in 1981, kicking off several years of rising sales, and this made it possible for the company to pay off its government loan seven years early. Chrysler was back as a major auto manufacturer.

Iacocca was respected internally and externally as a man of character, a trustworthy leader who meant what he said. His influence at Chrysler was transformative, overhauling morale from negativity to hope and corporate culture from shame and derision to dignity and self-respect.

When he stepped down in 1992, Chrysler was on solid footing.

Unfortunately, that footing started to give way not long after Iacocca's departure, mainly because the Chrysler corporate culture was so focused on him as president and CEO that when he left, the culture effectively evaporated. It ceased to exist. Without Lee Iacocca, the pride was gone. Within a matter of years, Chrysler had fallen back to its old ways.

Chrysler's story illustrates both the power of culture and the importance of infusing it throughout an organization, so that it permeates all levels of workers.

A company's culture must be enduring in order to stand the test of time. The culture must be institutionalized by making it the organization's culture, as opposed to the culture of an individual. We accomplished that at Cintas by teaching it, writing books about it, and reinforcing it every single day.

CHAPTER SUMMARY

- Documenting policies and procedures in an operations manual makes it possible to establish consistent processes throughout an organization. That uniformity helps reduce any variability in decision-making or execution. An operations manual can also serve as a training tool for new employees.
- Review policies and procedures annually to confirm that they reflect the current marketplace and environment. Update those that are out-of-date.
- Build in flexibility and adaptability by communicating that exceptions to policies are permitted and that it is an employee's responsibility to speak up when following a policy will be detrimental to the company.
- Corporate culture should represent all of the experiences and standards of an organization's workforce, rather than an individual leader's personality. Culture needs to be institutionalized to last.

CHAPTER 4

BASIC ETHICS

Many organizations overcomplicate the concept of ethics. Discussions around what is ethical and what is unethical don't have to involve philosophical debate and references to Aristotle and Plato. In many cases, ethics is simply doing what you know to be the "right" thing, the fair thing, or the appropriate thing. However, that doesn't mean that being ethical is obvious or easy.

Doing the right thing may be at odds with taking the most popular route or course of action, especially when the right thing is uncomfortable or controversial. Of course, more often than not, it's human nature for people to make decisions based on what's popular as opposed to what's right. Frequently, though not always, admittedly, they are two different things.

For example, giving direct, honest feedback to people is the right thing to do—the ethical thing—because in providing feedback about their performance, you're informing your employees about the likelihood of continued employment at your company or their odds of getting that promotion they've been eyeing. You're helping them see the reality of their situation, rather than taking the easy route and saying everything they want to hear, even if it's not true.

However, most people prefer to avoid confrontation or conflict and are much more comfortable providing only positive feedback. They want to be respected and liked by the people who work for them, so they steer clear of anything that could be construed as negative. And that's neither helpful nor honest and can lead employees to believe they are doing a much better job than they really are.

If you're more worried about whether the people who work for you like you than you are about whether they understand what they need to do to improve at their job, then you're doing them a disservice. You're not helping them improve. You're not helping them become disciplined.

HONESTY

Another aspect of ethical behavior is honesty. You're being unethical if you don't provide answers that are direct and true and if instead you choose to leave important facts out. This applies to issues big and small. Yet often being honest can be difficult and even awkward.

I remember one time when we had a supervisory position open in one of our distribution centers and one of our experienced employees applied for it but didn't get it. What upset her more than not being given the promotion, however, was the fact that a newer employee had. So she went to her boss to express her opinion that she should have gotten it, and he didn't agree with her. So she went to his boss, who also didn't agree with her, on up the chain until she landed in my office.

Although I agreed with the decision that had been made, I also wanted her to understand the rationale, so that she would keep giving her best and remain in the running for a promotion at some point in the future.

"Are you a Cincinnati Reds fan?" I asked her.

"Yes," she answered.

"Well, if you were the manager of the Reds and you thought you had a better chance of winning by putting in a young new shortstop, Barry Larkin, in the lineup than our regular shortstop, Dave Concepcíon, whom would you play?" I asked her.

"Well, I'd put Barry Larkin in as shortstop," she said.

"Well, that's what your boss has decided to do. He's not saying you're bad or you're not qualified for the job. All he's saying with this decision is that there is someone else who he thinks, today, is more qualified for the job," I explained. "And now you have a decision to make. Either you can either sulk about this and be upset or you can accept it and keep doing your best work, and maybe when another supervisory position opens up, you'll be the best person for the job then."

Fortunately, she accepted the decision and continued to do a great job, and four months later, when another supervisory opening occurred, she got it. But it would have been unfair not to be completely open and honest about what had happened and about her chances of landing a promotion in the future.

At Cintas, we assured partners that being upfront and honest at work was critical. It was likely you wouldn't be let go if you admitted your mistake or poor judgment right away, rather than lie about it or try to cover it up so that no one found out. If there is bad news, deliver it and deal with the consequences. That's the ethical approach.

SEPARATING BUSINESS AND PERSONAL AFFAIRS

In some cases, unethical behavior emerges because a senior leader has let their personal and business lives intersect. It's hard to remain ethical if your personal life is influencing decisions you make on behalf of your company.

Remember the CEO of Tyco, who spent $100 million of the company's money on art to furnish its headquarters? The problem there was that he did not separate business from personal matters. He liked being surrounded by beautiful art, so he had his employer pay for expensive artwork to line the company's halls. Was it in the company's best interest? Probably not. Would another C-suite executive have made the same decision if put in the same situation? Probably not.

You should not allow your personal feelings about something to cloud your decision-making. Decisions about the best interests of your organization should be clear. That's easier when you can put aside your own personal preferences and relationships in order to make them.

I'll admit that I was likely more concerned about this issue than my colleagues—to the point that if I brought home a legal pad because I needed a note pad, I would pay the company for it. I realize that's likely an extreme example, and Dick Farmer disagreed with me, telling me, "Bob, you work 80 hours a week. Why should you pay for a legal pad?"

My response was "But Dick, where do you draw the line? If it's OK to take a legal pad, is it OK to take a chair? A desk? A computer? Where do you draw the line? I draw the line at zero, at taking absolutely nothing from the company home for my personal use."

Dick thought I was nuts for being such a stickler, but I hope you see my point. If it's OK to take a legal pad home one day, can I make a habit of it? Can I take all the supplies my kids need for school? Can I photocopy materials for my volunteer role? When is it acceptable, and when is it not? If different people would draw the line at different actions, it's safer to prohibit everyone from taking company property home for personal use.

Given my concern with accounting for a single legal pad, you would be right if you guessed that Cintas was a stickler about complying with all governmental laws and regulations. Sure, there were some regulations I personally didn't like or didn't agree with. Some I even thought were downright ridiculous, but they were laws, and laws are meant to be followed. There was never any question about that.

Laws aren't optional, we would explain to our partners. If there is a law or regulation stating that you should do something a certain way, you do it that way. No exceptions. You don't look for ways to get around it or mislead people or lie about it. That was true whether a law had to do with standard accounting practices, hiring regulations, or any other law.

On the flip side, we also told everyone in the company that no partner should ever compromise their personal ethics or standards. It didn't matter what the company's standards were if they were in conflict with someone's own personal ethics; we never expected a partner to do something that went against their own belief system.

You may be crystal clear about your own ethical boundaries, but others may have boundaries that are wider or more restrictive than yours—meaning a situation or behavior can be viewed as perfectly ethical to one individual and not at all ethical to another.

Let me give you an example. Let's say you're a sales representative and you've just made a presentation to the purchasing manager at a potential customer that you'd really like to win as a new customer. It went great, and you felt like they were just about to ask, "How do we get started? Can we sign a contract?" when they get a message from their boss that calls them away from their office briefly.

You're left in their office, alone, on the other side of their desk. A few minutes go by, and you start looking out the window, then around the office, and your eyes happen to land on papers on your prospect's desk. You realize that you're looking at your competitor's proposal lying open on the purchasing agent's desk, with their quoted prices in plain view.

Do you look at it? Or do you look away?

When I've shared this scenario in business classes and asked students to raise their hand if they would look, I'd guess that about half the class raised their hands. As for the justification, I'd hear "They left the page open. She wouldn't have done that if she was concerned about my seeing it" or maybe "It's not a big deal. It's not hurting anybody if I take a quick look."

The other half of the class saw the situation differently, explaining something to the effect of "No, I couldn't do it. I'd be gaining an unfair advantage. It wouldn't be right."

There are many situations where two people can look at the same set of circumstances and view them completely differently. That doesn't mean that one person is right and the other person is wrong, only that we can have different perspectives.

To help people know what the right decision is for them, I tell them to go with their gut. "What's your gut telling you? How do you feel about it?" I'd propose as one measure of what would be considered acceptable or unacceptable. Your gut reaction, in many cases, reflects your personal belief system and morals. In turn, that determines what you should do— what is right *for you*.

SETTING BOUNDARIES

In addition to using a visceral "gut check" regarding ethical behavior, at Cintas we used a list of six questions to help partners determine for themselves what they were comfortable with. These questions included:

- Is it legal?
- Will I be violating a company policy?
- Does what I am about to do jeopardize anyone's safety?
- How will it make me feel about myself?
- How would I feel if my decision was published in tomorrow's newspaper?
- How would I feel if my family knew about it?

Although certainly not an exhaustive list, these are good starting points for deciding what behavior is acceptable to you and what is not. Of course, employers may have their own questions regarding acceptable behavior that you may want to check on too.

IS IT LEGAL?

This should be a fairly easy question to answer. And if you don't know the answer, you should be able to learn whether certain behavior is legal with a search of state law databases, a visit to your human resources department, or, better yet, a quick call to your attorney. In most cases, you already know whether something is legal. And if you're involved in a situation that potentially falls into some gray area, you probably still know the answer. If you're trying to find a loophole to justify your actions, that's probably a sign that what you're considering is, in fact, unethical.

WILL I BE VIOLATING A COMPANY POLICY?

Even if you're not violating a state or federal law, there may be an official company policy about the situation you find yourself in. And if you're doing something contrary to a company policy, such as charging personal expenses to your business credit card, for example, you shouldn't be. It's unethical.

DOES WHAT I AM ABOUT TO DO JEOPARDIZE ANYONE'S SAFETY?

At Cintas, we don't want anyone in the company to ever take any action that would potentially hurt someone or cause someone to have an accident. That means pranks that could cause physical harm are out of the question. So if the answer is ever "yes" to putting someone's safety in jeopardy, at Cintas we would say that action shouldn't be taken. It's not ethical.

HOW WILL IT MAKE ME FEEL ABOUT MYSELF?

This is the gut check. It's that sensation deep down inside—maybe you feel it as tension in your stomach, or a tightening of your shoulders, or something that feels off somewhere on your body. That's a reflex. It's your subconscious warning that what you're considering may not be the best decision. So when you feel uneasy, stop and ask yourself, "Am I doing the right thing?" Your gut may be telling you that what you're contemplating isn't the right choice.

HOW WOULD I FEEL IF MY DECISION WAS PUBLISHED IN TOMORROW'S NEWSPAPER?

Even if the decision you're about to make isn't going to become public knowledge, think about how you'd feel if it did. You pick up tomorrow morning's paper, and there on the front page, in big, bold print, is your recent decision. Are you proud of that headline? Does it make you feel good? Or are you embarrassed? Do you want to hide? Then you know what you need to do.

HOW WOULD I FEEL IF MY FAMILY KNEW ABOUT IT?

But even if the press didn't get ahold of your latest decision or behavior, what if your family knew? How would you feel about that decision then? Would you have some explaining to do? Would they be proud of you?

When you encounter a situation where your decision is unclear, run through these six questions to see where you end up. Let your conscience be your guide.

Yes, you should consider what your boss is asking you to do and what your company expects you to do, but, ultimately, you should do what your personal compass tells you is the right thing *for you* to do.

If that situation occurs, the first step is to talk to your boss about it. Explain the situation and your perspective. Ask for their support and try to come with a solution in hand, rather than just dropping a problem in their lap. That dialogue is so important, and, in some cases, once you discuss it, your opinion about the situation may change; you may decide that the explanation your boss has given you alters your opinion and your feelings about whatever you've been asked to do.

In the unlikely event that your boss won't support you, take your issue to your boss's boss. At Cintas, you could write a hotline message about it, to make sure it reached senior management—maybe your organization has a similar communications system. But never do anything that violates your own personal values system.

MAKING THINGS RIGHT

Sometimes you'll need to consider what to do going forward, and sometimes you'll come across a situation where something has already happened and now you need to decide what, if anything, to do about it. That happened at Cintas years ago, shortly after we began doing business with Firestone's retail tire locations. They had been our customer for about nine months when one of our partners walked into my office and told me, "Bob, we've got a problem."

The problem, as it was explained to me, was that although we normally charge a small fee when a new employee is being put in uniform, to cover the cost of putting new uniforms together, our contract with Firestone had us take that fee out. We built the cost of that prep work into the price. Yet for the past nine months, we had been charging the southeast region of Firestone a makeup charge for each new uniform. The Firestone southeast regional manager there had discovered our error and reported it to us.

As we started investigating, we learned that some of our locations had been charging this fee to Firestone in their region and other locations knew about the contract and had taken that fee out. Only the southeast region knew about the error, however.

"How much money are we talking about?" I asked him.

"Well, about $9,000 for the southeast region," he told me.

"And how many regions does Firestone have?" I asked.

"Around 14 regions," he said.

"Has anyone checked yet to see how widespread this overcharging is?" I wondered.

"Yes, we did," he said. "In the first nine months of our contract, we've overcharged Firestone $150,000."

So, the question was then, what should we do in this situation? Do we refund the southeast region $9,000 and hope the other regions don't find out about the error? Some people might. But not Cintas.

We had to own up to our mistake. Immediately.

I picked up the phone and called the president of Firestone. I apologized for our mistake, which had caused us to inadvertently overcharge them, and asked whether he preferred a check for $150,000 or a credit against future purchases.

Now, as it turns out, the head of Firestone's southeast region eventually became president of all the company's retail locations. Over the next few years, if he told me once, he told me 15 times how that decision to refund the total amount we had overcharged, even for regions Firestone was unaware of, caused him to be more loyal to Cintas than any other supplier.

Although admitting our error and apologizing caught the attention of management at Firestone, in a good way, we would have returned the money whether it helped us or not. It was just the right thing to do, we felt. That was a clear mistake we needed to fix.

But other situations aren't quite as cut-and-dried.

ELIMINATING CONFLICTS OF INTEREST

And sometimes it's possible to turn a conflict into a business opportunity. Like the time I was invited by our largest fabric supplier to play Augusta National golf course.

If you're a golfer, you know what a special opportunity playing golf at Augusta National is—maybe even once in a lifetime. Augusta National Golf Club, where the PGA Masters is played, is hallowed ground, just an amazing golf course. However, Cintas's policy about such invitations was that they weren't permitted. Suppliers couldn't pay for extravagant events or meals. A $20 or $25 burger and fries? Sure, but beyond that, it was not allowed. The reasoning behind the prohibition was that expensive events could possibly cause you to lose your objectivity in dealing with a supplier—to forge loyalties that would result in Cintas not getting the best deal possible.

Despite my strong desire to play Augusta National, I told our supplier that I had to decline due to Cintas's policy. "It's just far beyond what we would allow a supplier to do for us," I explained, "though I would love to say yes and really appreciate the offer."

I hung up the phone and went to tell my boss about the amazing invitation I had just received.

"Oh my gosh," he said. "Maybe we should make an exception here." Dick was also an avid golfer and understood what it would mean to me to play the famed course.

"No," I told him. "I appreciate it, but we can't do that. How can I expect the people who work for me to follow the policy if I don't follow it? I have to decline."

But Dick really wanted me to have that opportunity, so we kept brainstorming ways that wouldn't put Cintas at a disadvantage in negotiating with this supplier—a way that the trip could benefit Cintas. Finally, as we discussed the situation, we came up with an idea.

"Why don't you call the supplier back and tell him you can come on one condition—if you can bring a customer," Dick suggested. The opportunity to endear a customer to us, to give them the opportunity to play Augusta National, would be monumental.

So I called him back about bringing a guest, and he told me, "Sure, that's no problem at all!"

The next call I made was to the vice president of purchasing at Dow Chemical. It was probably one of the funniest conversations I've ever had.

"Are you available to play golf with me the first week of December?" I asked him.

"Oh, Bob, I'd love to, but there's no way. It's just such a busy time of year. We're working on year-end stuff, wrapping up the year, and I have to finalize my budget for next year. I'm just buried—just too much work to get away then—but thanks so much for inviting me! Maybe next year," he told me.

"We're going to play Augusta National," I told him.

Without missing a beat, he asked, "When do you want me to come?"

That round of golf gave me a unique opportunity to impress a customer and to get to know the decision-maker better, but that's the only way I felt comfortable going—only when I knew that Cintas would benefit from the invitation.

On another occasion, I happened to find out in passing that my younger brother, who was in the IT business, had sold some products to Cintas. I hadn't known about it, wasn't involved at all in the purchasing process, and had no influence whatsoever, but I wanted to avoid any suggestion of impropriety if anyone discovered that a family member had a contract with Cintas. I immediately went to Dick's office to alert him.

"Dick, I looked into this as soon as I learned about it. I want you to know about it, to know that the decision was made without any input from me, and it appears to be the best decision for the company, but I didn't want there to be any question about my involvement, because there was none," I told him.

Because I was upfront about it and made him aware as soon as I had learned about my brother's business having Cintas as a customer, it wasn't an issue.

The key with ethics is becoming familiar with your organization's rules, regulations, and expectations and then lining them up with your own personal values system to be sure they're aligned. If they're not aligned, you should discuss the discrepancies with your supervisor, to develop a plan for how to respond if you're asked to do something you're not comfortable doing.

At its core, ethics is behaving in a way that is in sync with your own personal values system—always—and understanding what your employer's values system is, so that you can recognize where the line between ethical behavior and unethical behavior is drawn.

CHAPTER SUMMARY

- Choosing to do the "right" thing often turns out to be the ethical course of action.
- Being honest, even when it's uncomfortable, is one aspect of ethical behavior. Avoiding confrontation or conflict by lying is, at its core, unethical.
- It's easier to make decisions in the best interest of your employer when you can separate business from personal affairs. Remove your personal preferences and relationships from the equation when making decisions regarding the best interests of your organization.
- Cintas had six questions we used as a guide for decision-making, to confirm that the choices we were making truly were the right ones for us.
- Sometimes your employer may expect you to take an action that doesn't match your own personal ethics. It's important to speak up about where you draw the line as far as your own beliefs and standards.

PART II
PEOPLE

Organizations have three constituents: customers, shareholders, and employees, whom we at Cintas called partners. Of those three, your people—your employees—are the critical element. Your success as an organization hinges on finding, hiring, training, and retaining good people. The Cintas Meticulous Hiring Process was designed to identify candidates who would best contribute to making the company even more successful than it was.

Bringing the right people on board is the first step in making the most of their skills, experience, and knowledge. To challenge your employees and give them the opportunity to contribute to the best of their abilities, you need to have a management system that tracks their progress and provides ongoing opportunities for growth.

Ignore your employees, or fail to provide those professional growth opportunities, and you'll have to grapple with turnover. Not only do you lose priceless organizational knowledge but also the cost to find, hire, and train a replacement can climb into the tens of thousands of dollars.

Focus on hiring the best and the brightest, then continuing to develop and challenge them, and you'll build an organization of experienced and loyal employees dedicated to your organization's success.

CHAPTER 5

HIRING THE RIGHT PEOPLE

No matter how great your customer service operation, you can't have happy customers without happy partners/employees. And you can't have happy shareholders without happy partners and customers. One begets the other. Your three constituents are all equally essential, but it all starts with your employees. Your level of success as an organization comes down to whom you hire.

I already held this opinion when, years ago, my wife and I had the opportunity to host the Women's National Basketball Championship for Xavier University, of which I was a board member. The University of Connecticut (UConn) basketball team was ranked number one, as they typically are, and were scheduled to play the University of Tennessee in the regional final game. Tennessee was the underdog, and yet they overcame the powerhouse UConn team in the semifinals to qualify for the Final Four. They then traveled to Cincinnati to play in the Final Four and won the championship. It was there that I had the opportunity to sit in on the press conference with the legendary coach Pat Summitt. In fact, Tennessee had won four national championships in the prior nine years.

In the press conference, one reporter asked Coach Summitt about the source of her team's great success the past few years. Without hesitation, she responded, "Simple. It's recruiting."

That statement holds true for sports and for business. Great coaches don't win many games without great players, just as great managers aren't going to be successful without great partners.

Finding, hiring, and developing great performers is the most important aspect of your job.

METICULOUS HIRING

You may recall the story I shared about when Cintas took the time to investigate why several managers had left over the course of a couple of years. Since our turnover rate was well below the industry average, it had concerned us that several partners had chosen to go elsewhere in fairly quick succession. Yet when we dug into the reasons for their departure, we recognized that they hadn't been a good fit from the start—meaning we shouldn't have hired them in the first place. We had missed some red flags that would have tipped us off that they weren't a match for the Cintas way.

What that exercise sparked was an initiative to develop a hiring process that would both find and hire great performers who were a good fit for the Cintas work environment and, subsequently, reduce the turnover that results when someone who is not a fit is brought on board.

The process we developed we named "Meticulous Hiring," because that was our goal: to be extremely thorough and meticulous, through every step in the hiring process.

This process had nine components, which included:

- Conduct multiple interviews
- Account for "must-haves" and "preferreds"
- Examine past behavior
- Ask pointed questions
- Check references
- Ask "stress questions"
- Define the answers you're looking for
- Determine culture compatibility
- Eliminate lukewarm candidates

Together, these guidelines added a framework that helped Cintas become more consistent in its hiring practices, starting with improving the rigor of its evaluations.

CONDUCT MULTIPLE INTERVIEWS

For candidates being considered for Cintas job openings, one of the most noticeable aspects of that process for them was the number of interviews required. Although many companies have two or three conversations with applicants, typically, we would have candidates interview with anywhere from six to 10 people within the company. Sometimes they might interview with the same person more than once too. That was true whether they had applied for a senior management role or a production line spot.

Sometimes those interviews took several weeks to complete, though we did work hard to condense the timing as much as possible, so that we wouldn't lose someone because they became so frustrated with the pace of progress.

Once all of the interviews had been conducted, we would bring together the interviewers to discuss each candidate individually. Typically, the discussions started with conversations about the overall impression the potential partner made on them, followed by observations regarding the answers the candidate gave to questions that were posed. Frequently, different interviewers would ask the same question of each candidate, to see whether their responses were consistent over time. Often, the answer given would evolve between interviews, so that interviewers had heard two, three, or even four different answers. We knew, however, that the first answer anyone gave was usually how they really felt about the subject. That's what we based many of our subsequent decisions on.

ACCOUNT FOR "MUST-HAVES" AND "PREFERREDS"

As part of the hiring process, we also had a list of qualifications that were required for each job and supplementary criteria that were nice to have. We called those "must-haves" and "preferreds." The must-haves were prerequisites that we would never compromise on, no matter what. There was no leeway whatsoever with those.

The must-haves frequently included years of experience and, for some jobs, might require a certain degree. Corporate attorneys in our legal department, for example, were required to have a law degree. For hourly production workers, in many cases a must-have was that they lived within a distance of the plant, which might be 30 minutes away.

The preferred qualifications were pluses. For example, an attorney who was licensed to practice in our state was a must-have, but a preferred qualification might be that they were also licensed in adjoining states. Or production workers were required to live no more than 30 minutes away to be considered, but it was preferred that they lived closer—within 15 minutes.

In the case of production workers, the distance-from-work requirement was established because we regularly saw that the farther someone lived from a plant, the more likely they were to continue to job hunt even after accepting a job with us. For example, if they had to drive an hour to work at Cintas, they would take that job offer until they found something that was closer to home, such as 20 or 30 minutes away. Before instituting that requirement regarding proximity to the plant, we had a much higher turnover rate because partners found it hard to justify driving long distances to make $12 or $13 per hour. Over the long term, they grew tired of all the driving and all the money they were spending on gas, and they'd leave. To reduce the incidence of that happening, we simply required a shorter commute from the outset.

During the interview process, we never compromised on must-haves. Even when managers reported that they were having difficulty finding candidates that met the stated must-haves, we insisted that they keep looking. Must-haves were a basic requirement, and preferreds were added pluses that could edge one applicant out over another.

EXAMINE PAST BEHAVIOR

In the interview itself, our focus was on learning about past behavior, because we believed that past behavior predicts future behavior. To better assess whether a job applicant might be a good fit, we needed to examine how they had behaved in the past.

That's not to say that people can't change, but, in general, most people will continue to approach situations as they have in the past. That's why it's such a good predictor of future behavior. For that reason, the focus in those six or more interviews was understanding what the candidate had done in the past, how they made decisions, how they responded to certain situations, how they felt about their decisions, and what they had changed about their behavior, if anything.

To get reliable answers, we frequently posed situational questions. For example, when interviewing a middle manager, I might ask, "What's the hardest decision you've ever made in your life?" After revealing what it was, I'd follow up with, "Tell me more about that. Why did you decide on the particular course of action you took? How did it turn out?"

My questions, or those of the other interviewers, were designed to better understand the applicant's thinking process. How do they think? How do they feel about their decisions after the fact? I'd want to know. To do that, I would ask questions such as, "Have you ever fired someone?" Then I'd ask for more details. "Tell me about that," I'd encourage them. "What were the circumstances? What had you done to try to help that person be successful at their job?"

My goal was to understand how each potential employee-partner approached situations and was likely to act the next time they faced a similar situation. I wanted to be able to predict their behavior, to assess whether it fit with Cintas's expectations.

ASK POINTED QUESTIONS

Direct, pointed questions were key to the whole hiring process.

I'd also ask employment candidates about how they process feedback about their own performance. I would ask something to the effect of, "In your last performance review, tell me about the areas of improvement your boss suggested you should focus on." Part of the reason for that kind of question was to hear what their boss was telling them about their opportunities for improvement. And then as part of the Cintas reference-checking process, I'd ask their boss the same exact question: "What areas of improvement did you suggest that Joe focus on?" You would be shocked at how frequently I heard very different answers from the boss than from the prospective employee.

The key here was to be direct and ask questions that didn't beat around the bush. If you want to know how they felt about their last job, ask. If you want to know whether they felt they were being challenged, ask.

CHECK REFERENCES

Now, you won't get very detailed feedback about former employees unless you go directly to their supervisor. To do that, you have to ask them for the name and title of their former boss. Then with a little online research, you can often track that person down and reach out personally for feedback about their former employee's performance. If you take the standard route to request references, however, you'll be calling the human resources department, which can only verify employment and salary level, at most. However, if you track down and call the person they worked for directly, you may be surprised by how forthcoming they will be.

In some cases, the information you gather from former supervisors can be extremely enlightening, as I found as I was checking references on an engineer we were thinking of hiring. He had previously worked at Procter & Gamble (P&G), and I was on the fence about him, honestly, not sure whether he would be a good fit at Cintas. So I wanted to hear how he had performed at his previous employer before making a decision.

When I called the former boss to learn why the engineer, let's call him John, was no longer with P&G, he broke down the typical career progression of engineers at P&G. "Bob, what happens at P&G is that about 30 percent of the engineers that we hire move up into management, even upper management. About 60 percent of engineers remain engineers during their time at the company, and the remaining 10 percent we lose."

"Where did John fall in that list?" I asked, trying to get a sense of John's performance.

"He was in the 60 percent," his former boss told me. That wasn't helpful at all, really. Yes, it confirmed that he was not destined for management, but was he a good engineer? I didn't know yet. I kept digging, trying to get an opinion out of his old boss. I asked question after question in an effort to get to the heart of the matter: would he be a good employee?

Finally, the gentleman started getting a little frustrated with me and my never-ending stream of questions. I wanted guidance, and I was getting nothing substantive. Fortunately, he decided to level with me.

"Bob, let me put it to you this way. If I had to row across the English Channel and I was allowed to put five other people in the boat with me, he wouldn't be one of them," he told me.

That was all that I needed to make my decision.

Keep in mind that reference checking was an important part of meticulous hiring and we didn't hand it off to a junior human resources partner to take care of. No, the hiring manager was expected to take care of the reference checking. The truth is a human resources manager wouldn't be as familiar with the specifics of the job and subtleties about performance, which is why I always did my own reference checks and interviews.

I also didn't give up easily when on the hunt for background information about an important hire. If I called a former employer and the supervisor I was looking for was no longer with the company, I would try to learn where they went or, if they retired, where they moved. Then I would keep hunting for them. Sometimes, when I told the receptionist that I had something very important to discuss with them and would appreciate a home phone number, I would get it.

Then I would continue my efforts to learn whether their former employee was one I wanted as a partner at Cintas. Even after two or three hours of interviews, I knew there was no way I could know a candidate as well as their former boss, who worked with them for months or years, did.

ASK "STRESS QUESTIONS"

One thing to keep in mind is that you need to ask questions that get at more than "What has your experience been?" I call them stress questions. They are questions that require the interviewee to really think about how they would act in a certain scenario—they can't be practiced in advance.

I remember one series of interviews I did on behalf of Xavier University, when the university was hiring a new athletic director. I recall a scenario I posed to one candidate that went something like this: "Xavier is a school that has graduated many basketball players, but we're very concerned about ensuring that the students are receiving an education, in addition to having the opportunity to play college ball. We rarely had a player that was one-and-done (meaning they come to Xavier for a year, play basketball, and then go pro)."

Then I posed the "what-if" question. "What if the coach came to you, as athletic director, and told you, 'I have an outstanding player. He's a McDonald's All-American, but he's made it very clear that he's going to play one year and then go pro. Should I continue to recruit him?'" I asked, "What would you advise the coach to do, knowing that Xavier is very focused on getting these student athletes degrees?"

He thought about it, and then he told me, "Well, I think I would take him. I would hope that we could convince him to remain all four years, once he was in the program. I would not want a whole team of people like that, or even the majority of the team consisting of players like that. But if we had one or two, I don't think that would be a bad thing. I would tell the coach to bring him on board."

That was a good answer, in my opinion.

However, in asking such questions, it's important to be clear about the type of answer you want to hear—what you're hoping the candidate will say. Knowing in advance what you're after helps you more easily assess the responses you get.

DEFINE THE ANSWERS YOU'RE LOOKING FOR

When we got down to the two finalists for the athletic director position, I brought both people in and asked them the same stress question: "As I see your job, there are a whole bunch of responsibilities. But the three main responsibilities would be winning, doing things right, and academics. What order would you put those in?"

The first candidate kind of fumbled, mumbling, "Gee, that's a tough question. I don't know . . ." I could tell he was trying to read me, to figure out what answer I was looking for.

Frankly, the answer I was hoping to hear was that all three were important and that one can't be sacrificed for another. However, the second candidate came up with an answer I didn't expect. He said, "Bob, doing the right thing trumps everything."

He was right, and his was a better answer than what I was looking for. He got the job.

Those kinds of questions—questions where you're trying to learn how someone has dealt with situations in the past—are absolutely critical.

After posing stress questions in the first half of the interview, in the second half I would focus on determining whether the candidate was compatible with our culture. Assessing whether someone was a cultural fit was just as important, if not more so, than whether they had the qualifications to do the job.

DETERMINE CULTURE COMPATIBILITY

Typical interviews ran two to two and a half hours long, which I hear was unusual for most applicants, who were more used to the 30-minute variety. At Cintas, we wanted to be sure the person was going to be a long-term asset to the company, and that took more than 30 minutes to evaluate.

During my interviews, I asked a lot of questions about people: I asked how they felt about customers in previous jobs, how they felt about the people who reported to them, and how they engaged those people who worked for them. With each response, I got a better sense of how well their experiences and behavior matched with Cintas's.

Most companies seem to spend far more time investigating whether an applicant has the qualifications to handle the job's responsibilities and spend little to no time on whether they are compatible with the organization. We flipped that on its head; we were fairly confident that we could help someone develop the skills necessary to be successful at their job as long as they had the same work ethic and ideals that the rest of our partners had.

ELIMINATE LUKEWARM CANDIDATES

Despite the fact that we had developed a well-scripted, exacting hiring process at Cintas, we were still wrong from time to time. Even after recruiting top candidates, interviewing them and hearing all the right answers, checking their references and receiving glowing comments, and then hiring them with great expectations, sometimes we discovered we were wrong. It happened.

But here's the lesson: when you hire someone you're lukewarm about—that is, who you aren't 110 percent sure is the perfect person for the job—you'll be wrong 100 percent of the time. Maybe one of the interviewers on your team wasn't as excited about an applicant as everyone else, or maybe one of the references wasn't quite as good as you had expected it to be, or maybe an answer you received to one of your stress questions was a little off. Those are all red flags you should pay attention to. They are small signs that you're right to be lukewarm.

Never, ever hire anyone you're lukewarm about. Yes, people do it. They do it all the time, in fact, mainly because hiring a new employee is time-consuming and difficult. On top of the fact that they're under-staffed, they have their own work to get done in addition to all the hiring activities.

As a result, many people rush through it, hiring the first person who ticks most of the boxes as far as experience and qualifications, just so they can get back to their own work.

It's human nature to settle for "good enough" so that you can be done with all of the extra work surrounding hiring a new employee. And yet, in doing that, you're setting yourself up to go through this process again very soon. You'll end up wasting even more of your time by hiring someone you're only lukewarm about.

Don't do it. Start over if you have to, but never, ever hire someone you have a reservation about.

FINDING THE RIGHT CANDIDATES

The Meticulous Hiring Process was originally developed in response to our calculations for the cost of turnover. We found that for the lowest-level employee, meaning the lowest pay—not that their job was unimportant—finding a replacement cost us $3,000 to $4,000. For senior managers, the cost was many of thousands of dollars; for a sales rep, the cost was around $100,000; for an executive, it was easily $500,000 or more.

And the process of filling those roles with the most qualified candidates actually started with getting the best candidates into the hiring funnel. We identified colleges and universities in different parts of the country that we believed produced students who were a good fit for the Cintas culture. And we would assign an executive to get to know the school and its administration. We had found that when you worked closely with a school, you could get the inside track on their top students. I know several times I received calls from a dean at a school who told me, "Bob, our student, Mary Smith, she is sharp as a tack. She would be a great hire for Cintas." And we would reach out to introduce ourselves to Mary, to start the recruiting process.

That happened only because we were a known presence on campus. We went to job fairs, we spoke in classes, and we attended campus events, so that the schools got to know us and the type of job applicant we were looking for.

Sometimes, when we recognized we were weak in some areas, we would make a concerted effort to connect with potential candidates. For example, at one point we had a big push to hire more female service sales representatives because we recognized we had too few.

So we brainstormed where we might find smart women willing and able to lift heavy uniforms. Some of the ideas included firefighters and softball players, so we began attending local softball games and handing out business cards to team members.

IN PURSUIT OF A DIVERSE WORKFORCE

Beyond gender, Cintas also understood that when you have diversity of experiences, education, outlook, and thought, the organization as a whole is better, stronger. When you have a diverse workforce, whether in terms of age, ethnicity, education, sexual orientation, religion, or geography, you make better decisions as a company. We knew that, and we worked hard to bring in people who were different from our current employees in terms of their backgrounds. It's human nature to tend to hire people who are like yourself, so when we recognized that our workforce was too homogenous, we made a concerted effort to diversify the demographics of our partners at all levels of the company.

We were especially interested in attracting nonwhite candidates, meaning Black, Hispanic, and Asian workers. We started at the college and graduate levels to find potential new hires, often working closely with educational groups, such as the National Black MBA Association or Prospanica, the Hispanic MBA Association, in the hopes of attracting strong prospects. We also discovered that particular universities were excellent channels we could partner with.

One school, Florida A&M, was a phenomenal source for us. Some of the tactics they taught there were outstanding for the development of business and networking skills. For one thing, they gave every new student a "nothing book." It was filled with blank pages that freshmen were required to fill with signatures from strangers. Of course, to fill it, they had to quickly become comfortable approaching strangers, from professors to alumni to visiting speakers, to ask that they sign their nothing book. It was an excellent exercise, and, perhaps thanks to that exercise, we knew students at Florida A&M would make great additions to our team.

But we were really always on the lookout for good talent, and we knew that the odds were the person we were looking for was already working. The waitress who served us dinner, the car salesperson, or the cashier at the grocery store—they could all be our next great hire.

We told our partners that anytime they witnessed someone providing excellent service—they were working hard and they were friendly, conscientious, upbeat, positive—they should get their name and number for follow-up. We expected all of our people to be scouts for top performers, in any industry, really.

With service salespeople, we also required them to spend a day out on a route before being hired. We'd pay them and partner them with an experienced service salesperson to see how they would perform. That was often eye-opening.

In many cases, we would hear back from our partner that we should definitely not hire the candidate they spent the day with. Although they looked perfect on paper, our service salespeople would give us an honest assessment of their on-the-job performance. Generally, when there was a problem, it was because the candidate was too slow, didn't want to work, or admitted habits that were unbecoming. "This is not the kind of employee we should hire," we heard from partners. That feedback was invaluable.

Identifying, attracting, recruiting, hiring, and retaining excellent partners were among the most important parts of any Cintas manager's job. Fortunately, the Meticulous Hiring Process, and the training that went along with it, provided a strong framework for building a strong team.

CHAPTER SUMMARY

- The most successful companies work to keep employees, customers, and shareholders happy, understanding that satisfied, challenged employees need to start that cycle and keep it functioning effectively.
- Cintas's Meticulous Hiring Process had nine elements that provided a framework for evaluating potential new partners.
- Because we calculated that losing an employee cost Cintas anywhere from several thousand dollars to hundreds of

thousands of dollars, as a company, we worked hard to retain our high-performing employees.

- Partnering with colleges and collegiate organizations was one strategy for recruiting a more diverse employee base. Becoming a visible presence on select college campuses created a recruitment channel that improved the diversity of our partners and helped improve the success of the company as a whole.

CHAPTER 6

MANAGING PEOPLE EFFECTIVELY

While nearly every organization would likely proclaim that its people are its greatest assets, too few companies actually invest the time in creating a process and a system to manage that asset. The well-managed ones do, of course, because they recognize the value that can only be created by leveraging the talents and knowledge of their workers. By managing I'm referring to a systematic process of providing feedback, identifying improvement opportunities, and offering education and training to continue to build the skills of each worker in an organization's employ.

One of the most useful tools for managing a workforce is the performance review, which is an opportunity to provide feedback and guidance to employees, to help them improve the quality and quantity of work they complete for the company.

PERFORMANCE REVIEWS

The Cintas performance review process was fairly regimented, to help provide feedback on a regular basis to each and every partner. Each new manager received a review after six months, after 12 months, and then every year thereafter. After a promotion or move into a new job, again, they would receive a review after six months in the new role and at the year mark from then on out. But the review process was nothing like the 10- or 15-minute meetings that many organizations counted as performance reviews. At Cintas, the discussions were in-depth and specific and frequently lasted several hours.

You might think that such a lengthy process was dreaded by our partners, and yet that was rarely the case. In fact, I recall one partner whose first performance review lasted two hours. At the end of it, he said, "Bob, I really want to thank you."

I was a little surprised, but I told him, "You're welcome. I just tried to give you feedback."

He said, "That's not why I'm thanking you. I left another job to come to work here at Cintas. I was there eight years, and you spent more time with me in my first review than my boss did in total during my eight years there. It just reinforces how you're trying to help me and make me better."

He was right. That was exactly what we were trying to do—help everyone improve— although I found that it frequently took two or three performance reviews before the individual truly believed that the feedback was meant to be helpful and that I didn't say things that might come across as harsh because I didn't like them or I was mad at them or disappointed. I spoke the truth directly and bluntly, so that they would know what they needed to work on to do a better job.

It was a team effort. The review consisted of input from several levels of management, not just their boss.

Before any supervisor scheduled a meeting with any subordinates, at Cintas they were required to first share it with their boss, to discuss the review and incorporate any feedback or recommendations their boss had to offer. Only after their boss had seen and approved it could they then share it with their subordinate as part of a thorough discussion. The performance review itself was divided into four parts, all of which were covered during a rather lengthy meeting: (1) A review of how they had addressed the opportunities for improvement identified during the previous review. (2) A review of all of the duties of the current job and how their performance measured up on each element. (3) The partner's goals and how they performed on their goals. (4) Areas they should work on improving in preparation for their next review.

1. PREVIOUSLY NOTED IMPROVEMENT OPPORTUNITIES

The first part of each review consisted of the three or four things that the partner was advised to work on—to improve—during the following year in between performance evaluations. Consequently, the first part of any subsequent review would consist of assessing how much they had improved on those specific points. Their performance on each was rated between 1 and 4, with 1 being poor, 2 being good, 3 being very good, and 4 being excellent. Of course, 2s and 3s were the most common ratings used, by far.

We purposely used a four-point metric so that supervisors would be forced to choose between 2 and 3 when evaluating their direct reports. That is, they couldn't choose a number smack dab in the middle, as we expected would happen if we had used a five-point scale. Nor could they use plusses or minuses; the rating was a straight 2 or a straight 3.

2. JOB PERFORMANCE

The second part of the review consisted of first reviewing the partner's job description. What were their responsibilities, and how were they performing in each of those areas of responsibility? Again, we'd use the four-point scale for feedback and assessment of mastery.

3. GOALS

Every partner at Cintas would develop between three and no more than five goals for the coming year to be included in their review. The goals had to be very specific and measurable too.

One of the mistakes I see most frequently with goal setting is that the goal isn't specific enough. For example, a goal of improving turnover within the organization isn't useful. How much does the individual need to improve that percentage in order to have hit the mark? If it improved one-tenth of one percent, would you say that they achieved their goal? They did improve it, but as a manager, you were probably looking for something more substantial.

The key here is to assign a quantitative value and a deadline. If reducing turnover is the focus, the goal might be stated as, "Your current turnover rate is 10 percent, so your goal for the first half of the year is to get it down to 7.5 percent by June 1."

That specific target and due date then become part of the review progress, to assess how well partners met the goal. And they would be evaluated on that four-point scale again regarding their progress toward achieving each goal.

4. FUTURE IMPROVEMENT OPPORTUNITIES

The last part of the performance review involves identifying areas for the partner to focus on between then and the next review. Those improvement opportunities also need to be measurable and specific.

AN OVERALL RATING

Keep in mind that each individual rating within each section should be able to be aggregated to provide the partner with an idea of their overall performance—meaning the average of all of the individual ratings should fall around 2 or 3, if people are honest. Sure, there might be a 1 here or there if someone is new to a role or performing poorly and maybe an occasional 4, too, in areas where they've performed exceptionally well. However, there were very few ratings at the extremes. Like a normal curve in statistics, most partners fall right in the middle. Those who receive an overall rating of 1 are given a short time line to improve or else move on to a new position or a new employer, and those who earn an overall rating of 4 are often fast-tracked for positions with greater responsibility.

Yet even though we expected most of the overall ratings to be 2 or 3, I can't tell you how many times I would read a review, see the section performance ratings, and be given the impression that the worker was a 2, at best, only to see they were rated a 3. We'd have a conversation after that, so that I could understand how, after multiple 1 and 2 ratings, somehow a partner had earned a 3 overall.

The reason for the higher-than-expected rating came down to a discomfort with giving bad news. No one wants to tell someone that they're not performing at their best. It's awkward and unpleasant, especially at the tail end of a review. So some managers worked to end on a high note, understanding that most partners really only care about that final overall rating, and those managers would want to give a number that was perhaps higher than what the partner had earned.

My job, as the supervisor's boss, was then to counsel them on why it was not in the partners' best interest to receive ratings they didn't deserve. In effect, we, the company, would be lying to them, and we didn't do that at Cintas.

Of course, that reluctance is human nature. Most people are afraid to confront another person with something that might be controversial or perceived as negative. Instead, they avoided it. But the only way to solve problems and make progress is by discussing them, out in the open, where both people try to understand the other's position. In a review, you need to effectively hold up a mirror to the partner and explain, "Here's what you look like to me." In most cases, you could eventually come to see things the same way.

When someone wasn't performing as well as I had expected or hoped, those were the toughest conversations to have. They were probably a lot like those some managers tried to avoid. The conversations went something like this, when I had to review Lucy, who had missed three of her five previous goals:

> *Lucy, you've missed three of your five goals the past two years. Now you have five goals again this year. I want to make this abundantly clear to you: if you miss more than two of your goals this year, you will not be in this job next year. Now, I want to do everything I can to have you be successful. I'll be available to you any time, day or night, weekends, holidays—whatever it takes. I'll send you to any training you feel you need, though I think at this point you've been to all the training that you could go to. I want you to be successful, because I don't want to have to go out and find someone else to do your job. So if you succeed in this job, it's good for you, and it's good for me. I want you to succeed. I don't*

want to have to put you in a different job because you can't handle
this one. But I need to be very clear with you. If you don't achieve
at least three of these five goals next year, you will not be in this
job next year. Do you understand?

When I shared this sample conversation with other managers, I could tell immediately that some of them didn't usually speak to their partners that way. They didn't because it was uncomfortable, yet not being as direct and honest was hurting everyone. The managers, by not being as blunt as they needed to be, would make the employee think that they were OK, that they could continue to perform at the same level and keep their job. And that wasn't the case. They needed to know they were in big trouble, and that might be what got them to change their ways—though I know these are difficult discussions to have.

Sometimes managers might even try to skip a review, so that they wouldn't have to have that uncomfortable conversation with an under-performing partner, but we didn't let that happen. Every boss had a calendar that tracked when performance reviews had occurred and when the next were due, for everyone on their team. If a supervisor didn't make an appointment to discuss their team's reviews, their boss would sure bring it up.

PROVIDING DETAILED FEEDBACK

In order to thoroughly review all the parts of our performance review, most meetings would be an hour and a half to two hours long. They had to be in order to address each goal or progress made toward improvement in certain areas. Each follow-up point or new area for improvement in the coming year required examples, sometimes several, in order to be crystal clear that the partner understood the level at which they were currently performing and how they were expected to reach their goal performance level.

The stark difference between our performance review process and the typical process at many other organizations was made clear to me during a conversation with the managing partner of Cintas's law firm. He revealed that they had just finished giving all their reviews the day before, to all of their staff members and partners. I was impressed, and also puzzled, because I knew they had dozens of employees. So I asked, "How in the world did you do all of your performance reviews with all of your people in one day?" I did the math in my head, and even at 90 minutes per employee, it would still have taken at least a week.

He said, "Well, they take only 10 or 15 minutes per person." That explained it.

"Then you didn't give them a review," I said. "You didn't talk in detail, in 15 minutes, about all the skills they've been focused on developing since their last review or provide detailed examples of situations to explain where they fell short and set goals for the coming year. It just can't be done."

Performance reviews weren't the only tool we used to manage people, but they were a synopsis of what they'd done in the last six months or year.

THERE'S NO TIME LIKE THE PRESENT FOR FEEDBACK

Of course, when you spot opportunities for improvement, you need to point them out immediately, on the spot. People need that feedback right away, so that they recognize when they've fallen short performance-wise or if they've behaved in a way that—unbeknownst to them—is counter to your organization's process. You want to stop them, point it out, and correct them, so that they can start improving immediately.

The last thing you want to do is watch someone do something wrong, whether it's responding to a customer request inappropriately or prioritizing their workload in an order different from what you'd like, and make note of it and only bring it up months later at their performance review. That is bad not only because they've certainly forgotten about the situation by that point but also because during all those months, they continued to underperform or make the same mistake, when all you had to do was address their performance right then and there.

When you give negative feedback, in addition to being immediate, it's important that you criticize the behavior and not the person. That is, don't call someone names; instead, comment on the action they've just taken that you want them to change. Those types of corrections might sound something like this:

> *Hey, Paul, I saw that you just hosed off that truck, which looks great, but you didn't touch the tires. Make sure that whenever you clean a truck, you hit 100 percent of it with soapy water.*
>
> *Sarah, I just overheard your call following up on an overdue invoice. I know those conversations are awkward, and you started off strong. However, I'd suggest that on your next call, instead of taking the word of the first person you spoke with, see if you can get a supervisor on the line. That's always a good follow-up request.*
>
> *Rob, I really appreciate your willingness to fly out at the last minute to see our client in Chicago. However, taking an extra day there without notifying anyone here that was your plan can't happen again. We were expecting you here for a meeting to update us. In the future, make sure you check that it's OK to delay your return before making plans.*

Although these aren't life-or-death situations, the same approach works no matter how serious the error. If you make sure the feedback is only about their actions, not their character or appearance or anything that could be taken personally, the odds of the correction being made without issue are much higher.

PUTTING ASIDE DIFFERENCES OF OPINION

Ultimately, it's important that everyone is in agreement about the way forward. There can be no internal disagreement, or there will be no progress or growth.

That doesn't mean that you have to agree with everyone all the time, including your boss. But you do need to put aside your insistence on doing it your way and follow your boss's lead. That was certainly true when Dick and I worked together. We probably disagreed with each other half a dozen times during my career. And even in those situations, we came to a resolution by talking through our respective positions. By sharing our perspectives, either I would convince him or he would convince me nearly every time. The seven or eight times we could not come to agreement in the 50 years we worked together, no one would ever have known. On those few occasions, Dick would tell me, "Bob, I heard everything you have to say, and I disagree with you. Here's what we're going to do." And that's what we'd do. No one in the company besides Dick and me would ever have guessed that we weren't in total agreement about that decision either.

That was important for sowing consensus within the company as a whole. We would never have wanted any partner to think that there was disagreement at the top levels.

LEVERAGING HUMAN RESOURCES INFORMATION

Once performance reviews were done, we would then update information in our software system. We had a human resources database that tracked details regarding every employee in the company. Each record contained every performance review they'd ever had, every training course they'd ever taken, their length of employment at Cintas, their current job title, their willingness to relocate, and other personal details that might indicate a match for future openings.

For example, if a partner were willing to relocate, but only in the Midwestern United States, because they had an ailing parent, that would be important to note within the system. Other partners might be open to going anywhere in the world, and we'd make note of that too.

The benefit of that system, which Cintas had purchased and then had customized, was that the database was searchable. Identifying potential internal candidates for openings when they occurred was quite simple. Finding qualified contenders came down to using the right search terms.

Anyone could use the system, so if a group vice president was looking for a new general manager, they could access the database and search for partners who had been with the company at least five years, who had been a sales rep and a service manager or plant manager, and who were open to relocating to the West Coast. Given those search parameters, the system would then present a list of the seven people within the company who met the search criteria, so that their personnel records could be evaluated more closely.

In instances where no partner met the search criteria, the hiring manager could adjust the parameters. For example, instead of a five-year tenure, maybe they'd be willing to settle for three. And perhaps a college degree wasn't critical. Cintas didn't focus too much on whether a partner had a college degree; a history of performance was much more important to us.

The only real challenge we had from time to time was when a manager was resistant to allowing any partners to be considered for other opportunities. It happened a couple of times, when a group vice president didn't want to lose any of his team members. When questioned about his unwillingness to give approval for a partner to be considered for a promotion, he had all sorts of reasons. In some cases we'd hear a variation of "She's not quite ready. She's really sharp, but she needs a little more time in her role before becoming a general manager."

This was the exception, however, as the majority of managers wanted to see people progress within the company. It was more common that if a partner was ready for a new challenge and a promotion wasn't available in their current unit, we would move them into another group where there was room for growth.

SUCCESSION PLANNING

One way to assess who among your workforce may be part of the next generation of leaders is to evaluate more than your direct reports, that is, go deeper in your organization, to get a sense of what skill sets and capabilities you have reporting into top-line management.

At Cintas, the CEO would spend several weeks a year, typically in the fall, reviewing everyone in the organization within two or three levels.

So the CEO reviewed everyone at the group vice president and general management level. And then group vice presidents reviewed everyone at the general manager and service, plant, and office manager levels, and so on down the hierarchy.

We used the GE assessment model, where everyone categorized employees as part of the top 20 percent, the middle 70 percent, or the bottom 10 percent.

Then we met to discuss those three tiers. The focus at the top, on the up-and-comers, was to confirm that we were doing all we could in order to retain those partners. Were we taking care of them? Were they getting access to training to help them progress? Had they been in their current role too long? What were we doing to prepare them for their next job?

We then took those discussions a step further, to develop a professional development plan for each partner in that top 20 percent, relying on their immediate supervisor to implement the plan and keep that individual building new skills. We wanted to ready those employees to move up and continue to be successful.

We also talked about the middle 70 percent, but not to the extent that we talked about the top 20 percent or the bottom 10. If there were partners who we thought had the potential to move into the top 20 percent, we worked on plans to challenge them and give them opportunities to shine.

When we got to the bottom 10 percent, we started by checking to see whether anyone in the bottom 10 percent this year was in the bottom 10 last year. Then the discussion moved to talking about why they were still in their job or why they were still working for us, if they consistently ranked at the bottom in terms of performance. We discussed whether the person was promotable under certain circumstances or whether we should just face the music and let them move on to an organization or job that would be a better fit. Sometimes the people in the bottom 10 percent had only recently been promoted into their roles and it was too soon to tell whether they could succeed; they were in that category because they were an unknown, not because of poor performance.

At the end of this exercise, as a company we had a much better sense of how prepared we were for future growth. We had identified our high performers and developed custom plans for each, to help them get the experiences they needed to continue to grow. We had plans to help partners in the middle 70 percent continue to build new skills and create the potential to move into the top 20 percent, and we had eyes on our bottom 10 percent, so that they wouldn't remain in that group long. We wanted them to either move up or move out.

We also kept a close eye on the diversity of our workforce. We realized several years ago that women and people of color (POC) were underrepresented and had few role models to look up to, so we made a concerted effort to go out and find high performers who weren't white men. We didn't hire them *because* they were women or Black or Latino, however. They were superstars in other companies, and we wanted their experience and expertise at Cintas. You don't have to lower your hiring standards to diversify your workforce, but you may have to look harder and in different places to accomplish that objective.

PROFESSIONAL DEVELOPMENT PLANNING

That several-week evaluation period was time well spent reviewing all the employee records. Conversations with managers about their direct reports were always focused on creating new opportunities for our biggest asset—our people. We'd brainstorm ways that we could help our partners build new skills. We'd look at their personnel records to see which training programs they had already done, and we might decide that sending them to Harvard for the executive summer program would be a good way to get them some exposure and teach them new management tactics. Or we might decide that it was time to give a partner responsibility for managing a high-visibility project from start to finish, so they could demonstrate their abilities and earn some recognition. People who were viewed as potential officers of the company were invited as guests to our executive committee meeting, so that the top people in the company could get to know them, see them make a presentation, and talk to them at dinner and at breaks. Sometimes we would invite them to corporate board meetings so they could see how decisions were made and who the top decision-makers were. That was especially important when potential successors to the CEO role were being evaluated.

BLOCKERS

One other aspect we looked at was how long someone had been in their current role. We would flag anyone who had been in the same job for more than five years. The reason was twofold: (1) if they had the potential to do more, we wanted to give it to them and not hold them back, and (2) if they didn't have the potential to do more, they were what we called "blockers."

Blockers were people who had reached the pinnacle of their capabilities. They were service managers who were great at their jobs but who didn't have the skills needed to become a general manager. But they continued to hold onto their job, which made it challenging to give up-and-comers experience at that level. Blockers prevented other partners from moving.

Blockers were often experienced, talented people, so we didn't want to fire them, but we did try to limit the number of blockers we had in place. For example, if there were four service manager positions, we couldn't have four blockers in all of those roles or else the upward mobility of lower-level managers was completely blocked. Two would be OK, however. And if we realized we had too many blockers at one level, we would try to make some lateral moves to break up the bottleneck at that level. We might move a service manager to a plant manager role, for example, to create some potential mobility.

Managing people effectively came down to focusing primarily on behaviors—on performance—rather than on personalities. We knew that 98 percent of the time, people will continue to do what they've done in the past, so you want to find and keep employees who were already performing at a high level. Sure, you could probably retrain the 2 percent, but that takes considerable time and effort. We found it was much more efficient and effective to recruit and retain strong performers from the outset.

CHAPTER SUMMARY

- People are an organization's greatest asset, and, for that reason, it's essential that a process and system be created to effectively manage that asset.

- A four-part performance review on a scale from 1 to 4 was one way that Cintas regularly gave detailed feedback to its partners regarding their performance. The review consisted of (1) previously noted improvement opportunities, (2) job performance, (3) performance on goals, and (4) future improvement opportunities.

- Although annual reviews were excellent opportunities for detailed feedback, it is important to immediately address any deficiencies or issues when they happen throughout the year. Don't wait until the review to bring up a recurring problem.

- Creating and maintaining a searchable human resources database was essential for identifying top performers and giving them new opportunities. Each partner's record contained previous performance reviews, experience, job history, and willingness to relocate, so that hiring managers could easily develop internal prospect lists for openings when they occurred.

CHAPTER 7

HOLDING ON TO YOUR BEST PEOPLE

The Bureau of Labor Statistics indicates that the average employee turnover rate nationwide, across all industries, has hovered around *45 percent* for several years. That large number should concern anyone responsible for attracting, hiring, and retaining skilled workers. In fact, holding on to top talent is a challenge within any organization, but the stakes are high. Losing high performers is costly, in terms of both brain drain within the organization and the additional expense that will be incurred in finding, hiring, and training a replacement.

Cintas paid a lot of attention to employee attrition and turnover, especially after we ran the numbers and saw that replacing an entry-level partner cost us, as previously stated, at minimum, $3,000 to $4,000 and replacing an executive could cost hundreds of thousands of dollars—on up to $1 million—because of the impact that a senior leader can have on the whole organization.

This focus on turnover emerged in part after I had the opportunity to spend time with the human resources (HR) director of the division of General Electric (GE) that was headquartered in Cincinnati. That meeting opened my eyes to how effective organizations evaluate their people.

One of the tools the HR director shared with me was a four-quadrant chart—essentially, a square divided into four smaller squares. On one axis of the chart was results and on the other was compatibility with the organization's values and culture.

People in the upper right-hand quadrant would be partners who produced good results and were compatible with the organization's values and culture. They were partners that we invested time and energy in retaining; we took care of them as best we could, including applying golden handcuffs. That meant offering significant salary increases, paying them above-market rates for their positions, awarding stock options, giving them access to and visibility with the senior leadership team, and involving them in making strategic decisions about the company's direction. They were the people we really didn't want to lose, so we made an effort to communicate that, in the hopes that having an ownership stake, being involved in important decisions about the company, and being well paid would make it harder to leave Cintas. We wanted to make it expensive for them to leave while also getting them involved in helping to run the company, so that they understood that their opinion mattered—because it did.

At Cintas, we used our matrix as a tool to help determine which partners were high performers and were a great fit with the company culture, but we never actually assigned partners to quadrants.

EVALUATING PARTNERS

Partners in all aspects of the business were evaluated annually based primarily on performance but also with an eye toward future potential. Partners who achieved high results and were a good fit with the Cintas culture were given plenty of exposure to senior management and a superior compensation and benefits package to try to entice them to stay.

People who were low performing and a low culture fit were easy to deal with. They didn't last very long. If they weren't contributing to Cintas's success and were potentially negatively impacting others around them with their poor attitude, we didn't want them. They were invited to find an employer that was a better fit for their skills.

Where it got complicated was with people who were low performers but a good fit. Although the knee-jerk reaction might be to let them go because of performance issues, the GE HR manager recommended giving them plenty of chances to figure out how to produce results. His rationale was that in the short term, it was more important to hold on to people who were compatible with the organization's values than to let them go because of lower-than-expected results. His thinking was that it's easier to teach someone how to improve their performance and almost impossible to teach someone new values and work ethic. Cintas had a similar view.

What was really interesting was hearing how GE handled people who were producing good results but who were not compatible with its values. Many companies hold on to these employees because they are performing. However, Cintas got rid of them, and so did GE, as it turned out.

The GE HR director explained to me during our meeting that within that last group of employees you'd find workers who were delivering results, such as a salesperson who consistently met or exceeded their quota, yet behind the scenes they would do things that contrasted sharply with their company's values in order to hit those numbers. They were incompatible with the culture. And many companies allowed them to stay, even when they found out about the poor behavior, because they were high performers. What many of those organizations didn't recognize was the harm that the staffer was doing to the company overall. Those sorts of people are toxic. They can damage the organization's external reputation and send the message internally that poor behavior is acceptable. The company will suffer irreparable damage long term thanks to this category of employee. Yet most companies overlook their flaws if they're delivering results. That's dangerous.

TAKE EVERYONE'S TEMPERATURE REGULARLY

One aspect of keeping good employees was checking in with newer partners frequently—what we called "taking their temperature." During the first performance review, which was after six months, I would take time just to ask about how things were going, asking questions like:

- "How do you like your job?"

- "Are you doing what you expected you would? Is the job as described?"
- "Do you feel comfortable here?"
- "Do you like the company?"
- "Do you have any problems? Is there anything going on that I need to know about?"
- "Is there anything I can help you with?"

We would spend an extended amount of time talking about their job in that first review: how they liked it, what could be better, or where they could use more direction or support. This was especially important with partners who we felt were "up-and-comers," because we wanted to know immediately whether there was something on their mind bothering them. We didn't want negative feelings to fester and turn into dissatisfaction. Instead, we wanted to know as soon as possible if there was a situation that could be addressed and turned around for them.

Our HR department was also involved in taking people's temperatures, since newer employees who didn't know their boss well yet might be reluctant to express their concerns to them but they would seek out someone in HR for advice. Given that preference, it's important to check in with your HR department to see what they may be hearing from employees. Are there situations that need to be addressed or newer partners who need to be reassured that they're on the right track? The HR department could be an invaluable source of feedback.

Fear of the reaction they might get to a question or expressing a particular concern is why some individuals avoided bringing issues up with their boss. They didn't want to reveal insecurity or a potential lack of knowledge, so they side-stepped them. Yet if they had known that tough conversations were always for their benefit, they might have been more willing to be forthcoming.

I can understand that reluctance, however. When I first started at Cintas, it was unnerving to have conversations with my boss, Dick—at least initially. He was an imposing figure, a taskmaster. It was easy to misunderstand his direct, assertive communication style as an indication that he was displeased with you or the work you had done, when that was rarely the case. I know that because every time he and I had a meeting where he pointed out something I wasn't doing, or that I could do better, the next morning he would pull me aside to check in. He'd say something like, "Bob, come into my office for a minute. Now, listen, I know I was tough on you last night, but do you understand what I was trying to tell you? Do you understand the importance of what I shared?"

He wanted to give me a night to sleep on what he had told me, to process it, and then to make sure that I had heard him and that I wasn't mad at him for telling me something that was hard to hear. He wanted to make sure I was OK. He didn't want me sulking or upset about the conversation to the point that resentment or discomfort would fester and affect my work.

Anyone who worked with Dick for a couple of years or more knew that was just his style. He had my best interests at heart, even though at times he would say hard things to me. Ultimately, his goal was to help me learn and improve.

That directness shaped the company's culture, which encouraged partners to speak up if something was bothering them. Everyone understood that if there was something on their mind, they should bring it up so they could talk about it and resolve it. That ensured that everyone was in alignment on decisions big and small, or at least they understood the rationale, even if they didn't necessarily concur.

The problem that can emerge if you don't address disagreements or differences of opinion as they occur is that employees may revert to talking behind people's backs—meaning they would point out decisions that were made with which they didn't agree.

That was the case with our head of engineering one time; let's call him Jim. We'd have an executive committee meeting and during the session make some decisions, to which he was a party, and I'd hear later that he would make comments indicating his disagreement with those decisions. Apparently, after a meeting ended, whether in the lunchroom or in conversation around the water cooler, Jim would express his true opinions. He'd tell colleagues, "Boy, that was the biggest mistake ever. I don't know why in the world Bob wants to do that. Not how I would have gone about it at all."

What he may not have realized was that those same colleagues would then come to me and share what Jim had told them. Because we worked so hard to be direct and honest with everyone, his negativity stood out. To clear the air, I called him into my office one day for a chat.

"Jim, I have thick skin," I assured him. "When we're sitting in a meeting debating something and you disagree with what I'm about to do or one of the decisions being made, speak up then. I want your input! I want to know how you feel—we all do—so we can be sure we're making the right decision."

Another of our mantras was "We don't care who is right. All we care about is what is right." We wanted to make the best decision for the company based on the information we had and the expertise of the people in the room. But if everyone stayed mum or kept their opinions to themselves, those decisions wouldn't be as well informed as they could be.

I told him that he needed to speak up when he had an opinion that might be in the minority. No one was going to get mad at him if he disagreed. We just wanted him to speak up and explain why he felt that way—in the meeting. After the fact, after the meeting was over, it didn't do anyone any good to have him expressing disagreement, I told him. "If you feel it in your heart and your mind that something is the wrong decision, talk about it in the meeting," I told him. I needed him to speak up more when decisions were being made and less so after the fact, when his opinion mattered little. I think he started to understand, though I'm not sure he was ever 100 percent comfortable with confrontation or conflict.

That was why Jim never gave honest feedback to his subordinates either. He avoided any kind of confrontation or conflict. And he didn't make it at Cintas, because his refusal to be direct and open about how his direct reports could do a better job meant he was holding Cintas back. He couldn't believe that partners would *want* to know the truth of how they were performing and how they could improve, because that would require hearing where they weren't performing at their best.

HOLD ON TIGHTLY TO YOUR BEST PEOPLE

Although Jim couldn't face what he needed to do to be successful at Cintas, there were plenty of partners who were superstars. Those superstars were the people we kept our eye on. We knew they could go far in the company, and we did our best to prevent them from leaving, going so far as to put on a full-court press, as they say, when we heard that someone was considering taking a job elsewhere.

That's exactly what happened with someone who was a service manager in Nashville, Tennessee; let's call him Charlie. Charlie was about five levels below the CEO in the Cintas hierarchy, but he was an up-and-comer; we had big plans for him. So we were surprised and disappointed when we heard from his boss, Pete, the general manager, that Charlie had received a job offer elsewhere and had accepted it. Pete called to ask whether he could bring Charlie up to Cincinnati so that the executive team could try to convince him to stay.

Charlie and Pete drove up to Cincinnati from Nashville one day, and seven different executives proceeded to sit down with Charlie to talk to him about his decision. The discussion was broad, but some of the conversations went something like this:

"Charlie, why are you leaving?"

"It's got nothing to do with Cintas," he reassured us. "I love Cintas. You guys are great, but I got this fantastic offer I couldn't refuse."

So someone else would ask, "Why don't you tell us about your fantastic offer?"

He proceeded to tell us about his compensation package and the boatload of stock options he was offered.

I pointed out, "Well, you have stock options here too. Do you realize you're walking away from a quarter of a million dollars if you quit your job here?"

He seemed really enamored with the stock options, so we at Cintas hit hard on that point, trying to sow seeds of doubt.

"Yes, their stock options are good, but they're going to give them to you at the current stock price. How do you know that the stock is going to go up?" We pointed out that the stock options he currently had at Cintas reflected appreciation that had already occurred; he had earned options at a lower price and had contributed to the stock price's rise. He had earned a considerable sum.

We pushed hard to try to get Charlie to reconsider, given what he would have to give up at Cintas.

In other cases, once we knew where the partner was headed, we'd learn as much as we could about where they were going. We'd scour their financial statements to find any sign of weakness so we could point out anything that might get them to rethink their plan. We wouldn't be entirely negative, but we'd bring up things we thought were suspect, such as "XYZ is certainly a good company, but have you taken a look at their balance sheet lately? Have you seen all the debt they have? You may want to ask about that." Or "Do you remember Donna, who went to work at ABC Company five years ago? She was there a few months and then came back to Cintas. Have you talked to her? You might want to find out what made her leave."

I suddenly realized that Pete had driven Charlie up to the meeting that day, which was curious. "Pete, why did you drive up here instead of flying?" I asked. It would have been only a 45-minute flight, and instead, it would take another five hours to get home.

"Bob, I got the guy for five hours in the car. That means I have five more hours to work on him," he told me. I thought that was genius.

Believe it or not, the strategy worked. Charlie changed his mind and decided to stay.

Another time, our CFO had received an offer from a company and had accepted it. He was supposed to leave Cintas on Friday and start there on Monday morning. The week before he left, we made sure everyone on the executive team had a chance to sit down with him and share their thoughts.

"You're making a mistake," they told him and then proceed to outline why he should stay at Cintas. We worked on him hard, bumping up his compensation to match the offer too.

On Friday morning, he walked into Dick's office and told him, "All right, I'm staying."

That was great news, but Dick told him, "Well, you'd better call the other company and tell them you're not coming."

"Man, that's going to be a hard phone call to make," he admitted, stalling.

So what did Dick suggest? "What's their number?" he asked. "I'll call and tell them you're not coming." And that's exactly what he did. "Oh, Bob's not coming to work for you," he told them.

KEEPING THE DOOR OPEN

Although we weren't always able to change a partner's mind when they had decided to leave, I'd say a good 25 percent of the time we were successful. Yet even when we weren't, we made sure to let them know that they were always welcome to return.

Their supervisor would say something like, "Look, you may think this new company is great, and I hope it is, but if you get over there and you find out it's not as great as you expected, the door's always open here. You can come back anytime. We love you, and we're going to miss you. We'll take you back in a flash if you ever want to return."

That often worked. Many times we would lose someone only to have them ask to come back a few months later. Of course, they couldn't come and go repeatedly, but if they left once, they most certainly would be welcome back at any time.

I remember sitting in my office one Saturday morning and receiving a phone call from Tom, a former partner. "Hi, Bob, this is Tom. I left three or four months ago."

"Yes, Tom, I heard that," I told him. "We were sorry to lose you. You're a good man."

"Well, I left because I wanted to move up and the folks at Cintas didn't think I was ready," he told me. "But things here are different from how they were at Cintas."

We ended up hiring him back in the same job he had previously held.

Another time, a vice president of marketing left Cintas for another employer, and less than six weeks later, Scott Farmer, Cintas's current CEO, got a call from him asking whether he could return. Scott was surprised to hear from him so soon and asked, "Why do you want to come back?"

"Well, I've been at this company for only six weeks, but someone here did something that they would have been fired for immediately at Cintas. But because this person is a good producer, the company looked the other way. I don't think I want to work for a company that is willing to do that," he explained.

Scott's response? "Well, Bill, why don't you come back here?" And that's exactly what he did—what he was happy to do, because we had left the door open for that to happen.

In addition to hoping we'd get those phone calls from former partners, we'd also reach out to check in with them after six months, by calling to see how things were going. It's as easy as, "Hey, Susan, how's it going over there? Are you happy? The door's still open here if you ever want to come back." Sometimes that worked, too, by reinforcing that we really did mean that they would be welcomed back.

CHAPTER SUMMARY

- The average employee turnover rate nationwide is 45 percent, which is an indicator that many companies are not being successful at holding on to employees. Holding on to top talent is especially challenging, because other companies are frequently trying to poach them.

- Cintas informally evaluated its workforce using a model consisting of four quadrants, to identify which partners offered the best combination of results and culture fit. It was a way to categorize them, but no formal label was ever applied in their files. Employees who were a good fit culturally were frequently given multiple chances to learn how to get results, while those that were not a fit—whether they got results or not—were shown the door. Culture fit is more important than anything.

- High-performing partners were given more attention and benefits in the hopes of fostering loyalty that would keep them at Cintas.

- When star employees announced they were leaving, Cintas went to great lengths to try to change their mind, including letting them know that the door was always open if they wanted to return. In several important cases, that worked at luring them back.

PART III
LEADERSHIP

Successful organizations are managed by great leaders, and I had the good fortune to learn from many during my time at Cintas. Some leaders were my superiors, some my peers, and some my direct reports.

In my experience, great leaders have nine characteristics that separate them from the average manager or worker. Those characteristics make it possible for them to earn trust, communicate their vision, and propel others to achievement in the service of the organization and its customers.

Part of being a great leader requires individuals to be tough, which is less about being mean and more about demanding excellence of everyone, including themselves. It's about having the hard conversations in order to help everyone achieve more than they thought possible.

Great leaders are also astute decision-makers who gather information and proceed based on what they know, rather than holding out for perfect information that will never come. They know they won't always be right, and they learn from their mistakes, vowing never to make the same one twice.

Truly great leaders have high expectations, and they do their best to make it possible for everyone in their organization to do their best work. Raising the bar of performance and then helping others reach it is among the most rewarding work there is.

CHAPTER 8

THE NINE CHARACTERISTICS OF GREAT LEADERS

Having worked with and for great leaders, observed many leaders—good and bad—and read many books on the topic, I've identified nine characteristics that I believe all great leaders have in common. It's possible there are other characteristics I simply haven't witnessed, but these traits are what I've seen that differentiate great leaders from lackluster or poor ones. These traits are also skills or abilities that are attainable through hard work and attention to improvement. They aren't innate or genetic, I don't think, which means anyone can develop them— and should at least try to.

THEY ARE VISIONARIES

The first characteristic of great leaders is that they are visionaries. They know where the organization is headed, or where they want it to go, and they are capable of describing exactly how their team can reach that destination. They can paint a picture that is both vivid and inspiring yet within reach.

A vision is how a leader foresees the future of the organization. That includes what the organization is trying to accomplish—its purpose. In its simplest form, a vision is being able to see the completed puzzle before it's been put together. When you're working on a puzzle, it's always helpful to have a picture of the finished product in front of you as a reference.

Many people refer to that picture frequently as puzzle pieces are put into place, to understand what's still left to complete as new pieces are added.

That reference picture is, in the big picture, what a great leader is able to provide, to help employees get a clear vision of what the company is striving for and what they're working toward.

Unfortunately, that vision is often lacking within organizations, which makes it difficult for employees to become inspired or to support that vision, when they don't have a clear picture of what they're working toward.

Dick used to tell a story about a guy who walks by a construction project where three men are digging a ditch. He asks the first worker what he is doing and is told, "I'm digging a ditch. What's it look like I'm doing?!" So he asks the second worker what he is doing and he hears, "I'm digging a ditch to handle the plumbing for the new building we're working on." When asked the same question, the third worker tells him, "I'm helping to dig a ditch to hold the plumbing for the magnificent cathedral we're building. It's going to have 12 spires and stained glass windows, and it's going to be one of the most incredible cathedrals ever built in this area!"

That third worker had the vision. He understood how his work was contributing to the larger purpose, the bigger picture. That means that someone in leadership had taken the time to paint a picture for him. The first guy had no clue what he was really working on. The second guy understood that his efforts were part of a bigger plan, but he didn't know what the finished product was going to be. But the third guy had the vision—because someone had shared it with him.

If an organization doesn't have a vision of where it's headed, the people within the organization have no idea what they can do to support its larger ideals or its plans. Having a vision and sharing it with the whole organization is key to being a great leader.

Dick was a great leader at Cintas because he made it clear from the start what his vision for the company was. We all knew that we were building a national company, staffed with motivated, competent partners, focused initially on the uniform rental business. Although there were a number of ways the company could have grown, Dick convinced us all that reinvesting company resources where we already had a competitive advantage—in uniform rental—made the most sense and would push us closer to our goal faster than expanding into new products and services, at least early on.

I saw the importance of vision at Xavier University, too, where I was on the board for 30 years and chairman for five. The president of the university, Father Jim Hoff, had a vision for Xavier that served as a metric. Father Jim's vision was to have every student receive a superb education, so that they were morally, spiritually, and intellectually prepared to enter a global society. Those were his words and his vision, which he must have repeated thousands of times. It was our gauge whenever we, as a board, made a decision. When we were deciding whether to build a new building, hire a new professor, or change some school policy, he would ask, "Will this result in these students receiving a superb education, where they are morally, spiritually, and intellectually prepared to enter a global society?" He would constantly bring us back to that vision.

However, having a vision isn't enough. Great leaders also have to have the ability to manage. Both are essential for success.

Some companies stumble by focusing on doing things right, rather than doing the right things. That's what happened to buggy whip makers when the automobile was invented. Buggy whip companies doubled down and focused on improving the quality of their whips, not realizing that quality mattered little in the face of obsolescence. Eventually, they were out of business, because they lacked vision. They were focusing on the wrong things.

Once you have the proper vision, you need to establish clear goals for everyone in the organization and an enduring culture that attracts good people and fosters an environment that produces long-term results. Great leaders look to the future to recognize trends that will impact their organization long-term, and they then make decisions to adjust the company's course, creating a new vision of success based on the changes they anticipate.

THEY ARE MOTIVATORS

Great leaders are able to motivate people, to get them excited; they are motivators. Whatever your political preference, I think we can all agree that Presidents Kennedy and Reagan were motivators. When you heard them speak on TV, you may have been moved to follow them.

One of the best motivators I can remember is Vince Lombardi. In the 1950s and 1960s he started and coached the Green Bay Packers football team, who rarely lost. They lost so infrequently in part because no player wanted to let their coach down. Vince made it clear that he expected his team to win every time. His statement that "winning isn't everything; it's the only thing" summarized his attitude about losing. He didn't want it to happen. Ever. And he instilled that commitment to winning in his team. He was well known for being tough on his players. He let them know that he simply would not accept losing, and if the team did lose, there would be hell to pay—and everyone would have to chip in.

He also made sure that they realized they were capable of winning. He pushed them to be their best as individual players, and together, they were virtually unstoppable. He was hard on them, but when they achieved or exceeded his expectations, he let them know he was pleased too. I remember hearing that when the Packers won the first-ever Super Bowl, he bought every spouse a fur coat and every player a new car. Every single one of them. And he told them he loved them.

You can be super tough as long as your team knows you care about them. If they understand that you're really trying to make them better, they'll respond to that. They'll rise to the occasion.

Vince knew how to shower praise on a player when they did something right. He would make them feel like the greatest player who ever played the game. He could make them feel higher than a kite, but when they did something wrong, he'd make them feel lower than a dog.

Great leaders need to know how to do both and to know which tactic to use when.

A good motivator is also willing to give credit for success to the people around them. They don't claim it for themselves; they point the spotlight at others. For example, when I was a general manager at Cintas and we had people touring our plant, I'd introduce our service manager and take the opportunity to praise that service manager publicly for their many skills and accomplishments. Likewise, if we had a good year, I'd turn to my team to thank them, telling them, "We just had a great year, and it's all because of what you did. I'm so proud of each and every one of you, and I love having you on my team. Let's keep it going and have another fantastic year next year!"

By the same token, when something goes wrong, great leaders shield their team from any repercussions and take full responsibility for any failures themselves. When we had a bad year, it was 100 percent my fault, and I made sure everyone knew it. I also expected our managers to take the blame, too, rather than try to point fingers at any of their crew. That's one way of demonstrating to your team that you have their back.

THEY ATTRACT FOLLOWERS

Great leaders are people others willingly follow. People follow them because they believe what the leader says—their vision makes sense to them—and the leader is credible. A leader explains what's in it for others. Instead of trying to convince employees to work harder so that the company makes more money, for example, they frame opportunities from the employees' perspective. Don't push workers to help boost the company's profits but, instead, show them that their efforts can lead to a promotion or raise or new opportunity for themselves. As a leader, you need to help those around you understand what's in it for them. What will they get out of working extra hard? It can't be only that the company will be more successful.

As a result of the company's success and growth, new jobs will open up, and greater internal efficiency means higher profits and more stock options for partners, not to mention rising stock values. Conversely, if everyone stops working as hard, revenue will fall and plants may close and jobs may be cut. No one wants that.

People want to work for a successful company that's growing, not one that's struggling to survive. It's easier to attract hiring candidates when your business is thriving, but leaders still need to explain what's in it for the new hire. People willingly follow leaders who are invested in developing their employees, in helping them to grow and advance.

One of the most impactful things a leader can do to attract followers is to pay attention to the little things. You've probably heard the phrase "Little things mean a lot." I take it one step further: "Little things mean everything." Noticing details and remembering passing comments that an employee makes are little pieces of information you can use to demonstrate that you care about them. For example, if an employee mentions that their grandmother is sick, asking how their grandmother is doing a few days later can have a big impact. It shows that you were paying attention and that the employee has been on your mind.

At Cintas, I always took the opportunity to call partners who were celebrating a work anniversary with us, such as after 5, 10, or 15 years of employment. It might take me a minute or so, but I'd pick up the phone to say thank you to each employee, to tell them we wouldn't be the company we are without them and that I'm grateful for all the hard work they've done for Cintas. Likewise, frequently, I'd write notes of praise to people in the company, to let them know how much I thought of them and what a great job they were doing. As CEO, Dick would write 8- or 10-page letters every few years, telling me how happy he was that I was part of the company. Don't miss those opportunities to make those quick phone calls or jot down a handwritten note to an employee. Those little things mean the world to them, just as they probably do to you when you're on the receiving end.

THEY ARE GOOD COMMUNICATORS

Great leaders understand the importance of communicating clearly and frequently—ad nauseum, in fact. You really can't overcommunicate when it comes to sharing a message throughout an organization.

Leaders communicate at all levels of an organization, not just to their direct reports and not just assuming that the information will be cascaded down through all levels with equal clarity. It won't happen. True leaders know that they need to repeat themselves over and over again to ensure that a message is heard, received, processed, and then acted on, when necessary. You can't say something once and assume it will stick.

This is one of the things that I learned when I ran the company. The last year I was CEO we had something like 25,000 partners. I knew there was no way I could just dictate a memo, issue it, and expect that all 25,000 people would be able to pivot on a dime as needed. It just doesn't happen that way. You need to communicate the same message over and over and over. You can't repeat it too much, to be honest.

This is especially true of your vision for the organization. You need to communicate the vision constantly. Dick repeated his vision for Cintas thousands and thousands of times, so that everyone understood where we were headed and how we were going to get there. The same is true of Father Hoff at Xavier. They used every possible medium of communication to share their vision and then help people understand how they could play a role.

Repeating the vision is like holding up the picture of the puzzle box as a reminder of what the goal is.

A good communicator also faces tough issues head-on. Rather than try to dodge tough questions, or talk in circles to avoid speaking the truth, leaders address them. I used to tell people, "There is no question you can't ask me. I may not have the answer, but I'll get the answer for you."

Good communicators also vary their tone and vocabulary to match their audience. For example, you may speak to people in your manufacturing department differently from how you might speak to your finance team or your marketing team. The lingo is different, and you need to adjust your language in order to be sure you're understood. Being a good communicator is a critical trait of a good leader.

THEY EARN TRUST AND RESPECT

Leaders earn trust and respect by setting an example of how to behave. For example, if you expect people to show up for meetings on time, you need to show up on time. If you arrive 10 minutes late, you've just demonstrated that it's acceptable to show up late. You can't arrive late and leave work early and expect members of your staff not to do the same. You're a role model. You need to set the example, to be someone others look up to.

Leaders also do that by not walking by problems—by recognizing and addressing issues that come up as soon as they spot them. That goes for something as small as a scrap of paper on the floor. As a leader, you can't walk by it and pretend you don't see it, or everyone else will do the same thing. You need to stop, pick it up, and throw it away properly, to demonstrate how others should also behave in similar situations.

Similarly, if you see someone doing something they shouldn't be doing, it's your responsibility as a leader—whatever your job title—to point it out. If I see someone doing something they shouldn't be, whether it's smoking in the office or taking printer ink home, I speak to them about it right then. It's as easy as, "Hey, we don't do that here. Here's why . . ." You can't walk by problems and expect them to get better. They won't without your attention.

You receive trust and respect by being reliable, by doing what you say you're going to do. At Cintas, if you weren't early, you were considered late. That was the culture: plan ahead to arrive early, so that if you encounter problems on the way, you still have a good chance of arriving on time. But you have to build in that cushion for that to happen. So just plan to be early.

Earning trust and respect also requires that you be willing to do anything that you ask others to do. Said in reverse: never ask anyone to do something you wouldn't be willing to do yourself. So if you're not willing to take on a cleaning task or a maintenance task, or even to address a demanding customer, it would be unfair of you to ask someone else to take care of it. You'll earn respect if you demonstrate that you're willing to do any job others have been asked to do.

THEY ARE FLEXIBLE

The best leaders also have a willingness to listen, to hear all ideas. They know that the only way to find great new ideas is to ask for them and then listen. Leaders want to hear what everyone has to say, not just a small group. Einstein defined insanity as doing the same thing over and over, expecting a different result. And so many companies do that. They are resistant to change, even when it is likely to determine their success or failure. Leaders need to be willing to change and even to look for opportunities to change for the better. They need to be flexible.

Likewise, people are generally resistant to change, too, and some need to be coaxed to jump on the bandwagon. They may need some hand-holding, which is really just more information, more explanation, more answering questions. But being willing to change, and even recognizing the need for change, is the sign of a true leader.

I remember when Sam Walton of Walmart was alive and most of the executives would be at the corporate office in Bentonville on Mondays and Fridays. However, he expected all of his top operating people on Tuesdays, Wednesdays, and Thursdays to be out in their stores and those of competitors every single week. Sam knew that the only way to spot change that's coming is by seeing what's going on out in the marketplace, by talking to shoppers, by looking at what's in their shopping carts, and by talking to employees, to find out where the bottlenecks or problems are and what they think can be done to address them. When something isn't working properly, ask the people doing the work what is wrong, because they usually already know what needs to happen to resolve the problem. You just need to ask them about it.

Great leaders are also willing to let their people make mistakes. Mistakes are learning opportunities, and the only way to improve sometimes is to fail. My favorite example is Thomas Edison. He was successful in developing the lightbulb on his 676th try. If someone had stopped him at 600 attempts, or even 100 attempts, we might still be lighting our offices by candlelight. But he kept trying, and no one discouraged him.

Good leaders are flexible enough to let people try new things and new approaches, even when they doubt they will work. I certainly would let people try something even when I was pretty sure they would fail. Sometimes I was wrong, and sometimes I was right. But unless they have the chance to try, you'll never know. What a missed opportunity that would be, for everyone.

I used to say, "If we're doing anything the same way we did it five years ago, it's probably not the right way to do it." Evolution is often an improvement, and you need to be flexible enough to try new strategies and tactics.

THEY EXUDE ENTHUSIASM AND CONFIDENCE

Good leaders have a can-do attitude and a positive energy. They rarely have a bad day or display a bad outlook. They always see the glass as half full, never half empty. They have confidence in themselves, in their organization, in their people, and in their future. That comes through as optimism and excitement.

There's a difference between confidence and cockiness, however. Confidence is a belief in your own capabilities and those of your team. It's a good thing. Cockiness, on the other hand, is bad. Confidence says, "We have a great company!" while cockiness says, "We're the best company in our business, by far." That latter statement suggests that there is no improvement opportunity—no reason to even try to improve, because you're already so far ahead of the game. Cockiness breeds complacency, which can damage an organization.

Good leaders feel positively about their own abilities and those of their employees.

At some point, as a leader, you're going to need to take charge. Sure, you should ask for input from those around you, but, ultimately, you need to be willing to make a decision about the way forward. You need to make decisions democratically, with plenty of input and counsel from the experienced folks around you, and then execute them autocratically—meaning, let everyone offer advice and feedback, but when you issue marching orders, everyone needs to fall in line and act on the decision you've made, whether they agree with it or not.

I've witnessed many leaders face employees who countermand their decisions, and then the organization fails, not because of a poor decision but because of a poor execution, because the whole organization couldn't put its efforts and resources all toward executing the plan. That type of mutiny shouldn't be permitted, in my opinion. Once a leader makes a decision, everyone should be focused on executing to the best of their ability, not questioning the merits of the decision itself.

THEY SET HIGH EXPECTATIONS AND STANDARDS

Leaders need to aim high, to expect a lot of themselves and those around them. As a leader, you need to have positive discontent and enforce high standards. People will usually exceed whatever standard you set, so make sure it's high enough. But people need to know how they're being measured or how their results are being evaluated.

To understand the importance of communicating expectations, I usually share a sports analogy, where I compare a boxing match to a basketball game. In a boxing match, you have two contenders. Neither one knows what the score is unless one gets knocked down and doesn't get up for 10 seconds and the match ends. Otherwise, they could go 10, 11, or 12 rounds and then have the winner decided by three judges from the sidelines. The feedback system in that sport is terrible. No one—not the audience or the contestants—knows who's winning until the match is over and someone else decides.

Now compare that to a basketball game. The objective of a basketball game is clear from the outset: it's to score more points than the other team. You can look up at the scoreboard at any point during the game and see how your team is faring. You can see how far behind you are and change your strategy accordingly too. It's the perfect feedback system; it's immediate, and performance metrics are clearly stated from the outset.

When I teach this as part of a course, I then ask my students, "Now, does your department or division look like a boxing match or a basketball game?" The looks on many of their faces tell me boxing is their answer, versus basketball.

People need feedback. You know that intuitively, and industrial engineers will tell you that if you just measure people's performance, you'll see a 15 percent improvement in productivity simply by keeping score. It's management's job to explain to people what a good job looks like and then give them constant, timely feedback on whether they're doing a good job.

HONESTY AND INTEGRITY

A strict adherence to a code or culture is what I'm referring to by honesty and integrity. It's doing what is right, what is moral and ethical. As I've said, very often, the right decision is not the most popular one. Great leaders are committed to making the right decision, whether it's the popular one or not.

True leaders never mislead anyone or lie to them. You've heard that "honesty is the best policy"—well, I say that "honesty is the only policy."

But I really believe that you cannot lead people if you don't care about them—the people you're leading. A quote from Roberto Clemente, the late baseball player who died helping his countrymen, mirrors my own feelings about true leadership: "Any time you have an opportunity to make a difference in this world and you don't, then you are wasting your time on Earth." I really believe that.

CHAPTER SUMMARY

- Great leaders have nine characteristics in common. They are visionaries, they are motivators, they attract followers, they are good communicators, they earn trust and respect, they are flexible, they are enthusiastic and confident, they set high expectations and standards, and they are honest and have integrity.

- These traits are not innate; they can be learned and developed. Anyone can become a great leader through hard work.

- One of the most important characteristics is being a visionary. That one ability—to conceive of a clear future picture of a company—then drives several other characteristics. But unless you have that core vision, few of the other characteristics can be leveraged to their greatest extent.

- Sharing a vision is akin to using the picture of a finished puzzle, which is often featured on the top of the box, to guide your efforts in putting a puzzle together. That finished product is the vision of what the puzzle, or the organization, can look like if all the pieces are put into place properly.

- The answer to a problem is never in your office. When you have a problem, ask your employees (partners) and/or your customers for input and you will find the answer.

CHAPTER 9

BEING TOUGH

Although the word "tough" has some negative connotations, I don't believe that being tough is bad or mean or negative. To me, being tough is a requirement of being a great leader. Being tough means being direct and honest, even when the content of your message may not be welcome. Being tough often requires that you give stark feedback—feedback that doesn't sugarcoat your opinion or feelings. The goal of being tough, however, is to help others recognize where they could do a better job. It's not to demean or criticize them—just the opposite, in fact.

Being tough is an attempt to motivate people to do things that they might not otherwise do or believe themselves capable of. It's about pushing them forward. Sometimes people can't supply the self-discipline, so you have to supply it for them. Being tough is also an indication that you care, that you know that someone else is able to accomplish more than they currently are and you want to support them.

If you work for a boss who is demanding, but not unreasonable, you will accomplish more than if you work for a boss who does not require your best work. Tough bosses stretch you; they push you to achieve more, because they know you can. And the art of being a good manager is learning how to stretch people without breaking them—to help them initiate positive change.

Part of the challenge of being tough is convincing your team members, your employees or partners, that you care about them and that the point of your being tough is to make them better. Otherwise, your toughness can spark a negative reaction, not a positive one, and that is more likely to lead to disengagement and resentment, neither of which you want.

I describe this process as feedback, as if you're holding up a mirror in front of someone and showing them how they appear to you, saying, "This is what you really look like. You may not realize that you sometimes look like this, but here is your reality. This is an area where you can improve, and here's how you can get started."

Human nature is such that most people avoid situations that are likely to be unpleasant, such as conversations that could turn into a conflict. And when you're being tough with someone, that discussion could turn confrontational; it doesn't have to, but it could. How the discussion is resolved depends both on how you, as the boss, approach your employee and on how the employee receives the feedback you're offering. When it is understood that the information is shared with the intent to help the employee improve and grow, the outcome can be very positive. But when the employee feels the feedback is unfair or unwarranted, the dynamic can turn angry or frustrated. Then you become the enemy.

HONESTY IS THE BEST POLICY

If leaders refuse to allow such discussions to become confrontational by completely sugarcoating the feedback they need to give, no one wins. Sure, they avoid any sort of conflict, but the employee turns away from that conversation assuming they're doing a great job when, in reality, there is room for improvement—only, the employee doesn't know that because their boss chose to avoid being tough. Their boss hasn't communicated the message they really need to, in that case, and that's not fair to the employee.

To try to make the case for having those tough conversations with employees, I'll ask managers, "Wouldn't you prefer that your boss tell you how they really feel about you and your performance and not sugarcoat it? Because it's likely that they'll go back to *their* boss and share how they really feel about you. Wouldn't you want to hear the same things that their boss is hearing about you?"

If you sugarcoat feedback, you're shortchanging your employee. By telling them they're doing a great job and not helping them see the opportunities for improvement, they won't strive to get better. They aren't aware of their weaknesses and don't know they have skills they should be working on. That's one way that you're shortchanging them with sugarcoating feedback.

More important, however, is that you're effectively lying to them. You're misleading them into believing that they're doing a better job than they really are. In doing so, you're actually putting them in a dangerous career situation. Because if their performance is weak but they have no idea, they are at risk of being demoted or fired. You're not giving them the chance to better themselves or their performance by pretending they're already doing a great job.

The worst thing a manager can do is not be honest and straightforward with employees about their performance, because it can lead workers to believe that they're doing a better job than they are. They're in trouble, and they don't know it. What's worse is they could be fired, and they would be caught by surprise, because they had no clue that they were at risk of being let go for poor performance. They're left in total shock, which is unfair to them, since it was their boss who wasn't honest about how their performance stacked up. They weren't given a chance to do their best.

PROVIDING EFFECTIVE FEEDBACK

As I've mentioned before, to be effective, feedback needs to be immediate—good or bad. Employees need to be told right away when they've done something wrong, as well as when they've done a great job. Immediate feedback ensures that either they know they need to change their ways, if they've done something incorrectly, or they know what they just did was well received and they should attempt that behavior more often. Immediate feedback is an opportunity to take corrective action right away, rather than let the bad behavior continue beyond that point, as well as to encourage better decision-making going forward.

When providing feedback that isn't entirely positive, such as after you've discovered a mistake or observed an ethical lapse, it's important to criticize the behavior and not the individual. Address what they did, not who they are or what may have led them to take a particular course of action.

For example, you should never start a conversation with something like, "You idiot, what in the world is wrong with you?!" Insulting someone or putting them down immediately puts them on the defensive and makes it almost impossible for them to hear the actual guidance you want to impart—the instruction regarding what to do differently.

Don't attack the person, such as with name-calling, but rather address the steps they took that were not optimal or appropriate. A better approach than leading with "You dummy …" would be to say, "Hey, Jim, can we talk about how you dealt with Sue over at ABC Corporation?" After identifying the situation or scenario, you can proceed to dissect what went wrong, such as, "It's clear you were angry with her. I assume that she must have done something that really set you off, and you're probably justified in being mad, but you can never yell at customers. Ever. Yelling isn't something that we tolerate. You can yell once you're back in your car all alone and a few miles down the road, but I don't want to ever hear about you yelling at anyone else in public. Understand?"

Or you might say, "Dawn, this morning in our meeting, you said [something], which was inappropriate. You should not have said that, and here's why." After pinpointing the errant behavior, you can then get into what they could have done differently and then reinforce that you still think highly of them as a person. For example, you could say, "Dawn, I know you're a smart, caring person, but you came across as very uncaring in that situation." Again, I'm holding that mirror up so the employee can recognize how they came across to others. I usually finish with something encouraging and positive, such as, "I know you're better than that, so just be careful in the future. Think about what you're going to say before you say it."

In a nutshell, those conversations should include:

- Here is what you did.
- Here is why it was wrong or inappropriate.
- Here is what you should have or could have done.
- I know you can do better in the future.

Of course, the absolute worst thing you can do is ignore bad behavior and fail to address it.

WE ALL STUMBLE

Of course, I've been on the receiving end of that kind of feedback too. I remember the first time I presented to a customer and I told them, "You have this problem." I was direct and honest, and immediately after that meeting Dick pulled me aside to talk about how I did.

"Bob, never tell a customer that they have a problem—come at it from the side," he said.

"What do you mean?" I asked, unfamiliar with that tactic.

He called it the "fair find approach." It was essentially a template for introducing an idea that didn't exactly point any fingers at the customer that could make them defensive. Dick explained that such a conversation could sound like this:

> I don't know if you have this problem, but many of our custom-
> ers who have had similar situations have found that this was
> the issue. Now, you may or may not have this problem, but here
> is how we fixed it for other customers . . .

This is one way to bring up the possibility of a particular problem without making the customer feel as if you are criticizing them. That's how you come at it from the side: "other people have encountered this situation and found that xyz works . . ." It's much less accusatory and keeps the conversation focused on the solution, rather than what may have caused the situation in the first place.

TRUST TAKES TIME

It's important to make sure that customers understand that you're not putting them down, just as it's important to convey that to employees. And when you have a new employee, it will take time before they truly trust you as a boss, or at least trust that your goal is to help them improve as an employee. In my experience, it took at least a year for a subordinate to know that when I was tough on them, or when I corrected them or was seemingly hard on them, it was because I had high hopes for their future with the company. It took many months for new employees to believe that I cared about them and that I wanted them to be successful; I didn't enjoy having conversations with them about their weaknesses or missteps, but that was necessary if they were going to understand how to do a better job.

Many new employees were pretty stunned by the blunt feedback they'd receive in their first review at Cintas, because they weren't used to such detailed observations about what they had done and how they could improve. It was tough for them to hear initially, but over time it started to sink in that managers sincerely wanted to see them grow professionally and succeed, and the only way to do that was to continue to improve their skills and abilities. The only way *that* was going to happen was if their boss voiced their concerns and insights.

Of course, before any tough performance review, managers would run through the feedback they intended to give, trying out language they were going to use with their boss, like a trial run. Then, once the review was completed, they'd go back to their boss to report on how the subordinate took the information and how the conversation went. Their boss might ask, "How did it go? What did they say? What did you say to that? Do you think you got through to them?"

HEARING FROM THE BOSS'S BOSS

In some cases, I would have my subordinate meet with my boss, because the employee was skeptical of the feedback I had shared. If they pushed back, telling me, "Bob, I don't think you're right about that," I would ask my boss to talk with them, to reinforce what I was trying to convey. At Cintas, we set up those meetings whenever there was disbelief or resistance to hearing what an immediate supervisor was trying to impart.

I recall one time I had to be super tough. I had to be someone's boss's boss and step in to try to reinforce a major behavior change, so that we wouldn't have to let the employee go.

The situation emerged after Cintas bought a good-sized company in Chicago, in early 2000. There were good people there, including the manager of the distribution center; let's call him Bill. However, Bill was a smoker, we discovered. At Cintas, we did our best to help employees, and especially senior partners, to quit smoking. It's not healthy, and we didn't want to lose this terrific employee due to health issues that were bound to crop up later as a result of his smoking.

So I sat down with Bill's boss, Michael, and told him that he should talk to Bill and explain why Bill needed to stop smoking. I emphasized how important it was that we get Bill to stop. Michael seemed to understand.

Three or four months later, when I was back in Chicago, I saw Bill outside smoking a cigarette. I was surprised, because I was pretty sure I had been clear to Michael about the tough conversation that needed to happen. So I called Michael to find out what had happened.

"Did you talk to Bill about stopping smoking?" I asked.

"Yes, I've talked to him two or three times," Michael told me.

"Well, he's still smoking," I told him. "I just came in from the parking lot, and he's outside having a cigarette."

"Yeah, I know. I just haven't been able to get through to him," Michael admitted.

"Well, we're going to have to get through to him," I said, and asked Michael to set up a meeting with Bill. In that meeting, I knew I was going to have to be extremely tough—bordering on harsh—because smoking is an extremely difficult addiction to break. But I had to try to get through, for Bill's sake and ours.

Bill walked into the meeting, and I immediately asked him about his smoking. "Bill, has Michael talked to you on several occasions about not smoking?" I asked.

"Yes," he said, sheepishly.

"Well, then why are you still smoking?" I pushed.

He tried to dance around the issue, suggesting he was cutting back, but I wouldn't hear it.

"Bill, don't lie to me. I saw you smoking when I came in yesterday," I told him.

"It's hard to do, Bob," he admitted. "It's a nasty habit, and I'm trying to quit, but it's just not working."

"Well, Bill, I'm going to say some very hard things to you right now, and you may not like me after I get done saying what I'm about to say, but I want you to know I say it because I care about you," I told him. "You're doing a great job here, and I think you have the potential to do even more. And when I see someone with such terrific potential smoking cigarettes, I know they're probably going to get cancer. And even if they don't get cancer, cigarettes damage their health, which means they're not going to be working for us long. So I'm speaking out to help you see the damage you're doing to your health and your career."

Then I asked, "Bill, do you have a cigarette?" He pulled out a pack.

"Give me one," I asked him, and then held it between my thumb and index finger in front of his face.

"Bill, let me tell you about this thing right here. It owns you. It's bigger than you. It's stronger than you. It's tougher than you. It's going to cause you to be in an oxygen tent someday. Ten or 20 years from now, your family is going to have to come visit you in the hospital, in the oxygen tent, and you may not even be able to talk to them, because of this thing right here," I said.

I went on for about 45 minutes, underscoring how his life was going to go radically downhill if he didn't take the opportunity right now to stop smoking.

Then I told him, "Bill, as I said at the beginning of this meeting, I say these things to you to try to provide the motivation you may need to stop smoking. I say these things because I care about you, because I think you're a good man, and because you're doing a lot of wonderful things inside this company, but if you don't beat this little thing right here, you're going to pay a big price in the future."

Bill walked out of that meeting and never touched another cigarette. Four months later he was running marathons. To this day, if he's thanked me once, he's thanked me hundreds of times for that tough conversation.

Although being tough was hard for me and I certainly didn't enjoy it, I knew I had to provide the discipline for Bill that he couldn't supply himself at that point.

In another case, I fired someone because he was becoming increasingly unreliable; let's call him Bruce. Something wasn't right, and Bruce's performance had nosedived. I warned him for two years that he needed to make some changes, and he never did, so I fired him. It was very unpleasant, and I felt bad about it, but I couldn't get him to make the changes he needed to make.

Many years later, I received a phone call from Bruce asking whether he could come meet with me. I thought it was odd, but I agreed. As soon as he walked into my office, Bruce broke down crying, thanking me for firing him.

I was puzzled, so I asked him why he would thank me for being fired.

"Bob, I was an alcoholic and didn't realize it, and when you fired me, it shook me up so bad that I quit drinking and joined Alcoholics Anonymous. I never would have done that if you hadn't fired me," he told me.

Granted, that was the only time anyone came back to me and thanked me for firing them, but that reinforced to me that being tough could have very positive consequences. No matter how uncomfortable or unpleasant it was for me, providing that feedback to employees was essential—for their sake. I made a difference in someone's life because

I was willing to give them tough love. You can have the same impact if you're willing to be tough too.

You also have to know when to back off of being tough. I had one partner who was a high performer who had worked for me for years. Then all of a sudden, his performance started slipping—badly. It was noticeable, so I got tough with him, trying to discipline him to improve.

Then I learned he was going through a difficult divorce. Although I've never personally been through one, one of my kids has, and I know they can tear people up. It's an extremely stressful time that makes it difficult to do much of anything, especially if you have to fight it out through lawyers.

Once I learned the source of his downturn, I backed off. For about six months, I stood on the sidelines as he worked through his divorce. Had I been my normal self, I probably would have fired him, or I would have been so hard on him that he would have quit. But by giving him space to work through all that was going on in his personal life, I allowed him to get back to normal eventually.

While some situations require you to step in and be tough, demanding better performance, that isn't always the right call. You have to use judgment, recognizing that there can be extenuating circumstances. When an employee loses their mother or their father, or deals with a personal tragedy of some kind, getting tough with them won't help at all; it will only hurt. And if your true goal is to help them because you care about them, sometimes you need to back off and let them know they have your support, through whatever it is they're dealing with.

Even if an employee doesn't approach you to reveal what's going on in their personal life, if you have a close enough relationship with them, you could ask what's been going on. You could start with an observation, such as, "Ruth, this isn't like you. You've been a great performer for so many years, but lately you haven't been yourself. Is there something going on? Maybe something in your personal life or something else that's causing you to act this way? Because you're not acting like you." Gently probe for an explanation. When I did, it was rare that the employee didn't open up about what was going on outside of work.

When employees know that you sincerely care about their well-being, it's very likely they will open up to you. So when I did probe, it didn't take much encouragement for employees to be straight with me. When they did, I backed off, rather than trying to turn the screw tighter to force performance improvements. If they were battling outside issues, whether it was mental health or substance abuse or a personal relationship gone wrong, becoming tougher would not have had the desired results and would have risked pushing them to quit out of frustration.

Being tough and supplying the self-discipline temporarily to someone who's struggling to make an important change in their life can make it possible for improvement to occur. However, at some point, that employee needs to take personal responsibility for their life and their behaviors. Being tough with them can jumpstart personal discipline, but eventually, you need to back away and let the employee take the needed steps to change their behavior. You can't do it for them.

CHAPTER SUMMARY

- Being tough is not the same as being mean or mad. Being tough involves being direct and honest with others, even when your message isn't pleasant or welcome. Providing honest, straightforward feedback is the key to sparking important behavior changes in employees.
- By being tough, you attempt to motivate a good employee to do things they might not have believed they were capable of. You push them forward, providing temporary self-discipline they need to attempt a difficult feat, whether it's quitting smoking or getting to work on time every day.
- Bosses who are tough are actually demonstrating that they care about their employees and that they believe they are

very capable. Being tough with them, to push them to better performance, is a sign that they are confident that their employees have the potential to be high performers. Bosses who aren't tough are not demanding the best work, and everyone suffers as a result.

• Tough conversations are rarely pleasant, but they're very important. When offering constructive criticism, tell the employee what they did, why it was wrong, and what they should have done instead and reassure them that you have faith that they can do better.

CHAPTER 10

LEARNING FROM MISTAKES

We all make mistakes. They're a given. Honestly, I don't worry about people making mistakes. When I worry is when I see someone making the same mistake over and over, which tells me either they aren't listening or they're not smart enough to realize they're making a mistake. Too many people are so focused on formulating a response to what someone is telling them that they don't hear the content, or the meaning, of what was shared, which makes them prone to mistakes. The only people who don't make mistakes are the folks who aren't doing anything.

When you do make a mistake, the next step should be to simply admit it. Don't try to place blame for the misstep elsewhere or come up with excuses for why it occurred. There's no shame in trying something that didn't work or in simply doing something wrong. It happens to all of us. Unfortunately, there is such pressure today to be right, and that can become a problem.

One of the many sayings we had at Cintas was "We don't care who is right. All we care about is what is right."

MAKING GOOD DECISIONS

To make smart decisions and avoid mistakes, you need information. You need input. However, you should approach big decisions and little decisions differently, and not everyone does. One of the mistakes I see people making with respect to little decisions is in wanting too much information. They want to know as much as possible before making what comes down to a trivial decision. As a result, they'll spend way too much time researching and collecting opinions about decisions that will likely have little to no impact on their careers or quality of life, such as adding a new product or service or selecting the colors in their office.

Little decisions don't require perfect information. You should be able to make a decent decision on small matters with 70 or 80 percent of information available—information you gather in a few short minutes. Just make the decision and move on to more pressing issues. If you make a mistake with your decision, it will probably be easy to backtrack and correct it or continue on accepting the trivial choice you made. With little decisions, a wrong decision will often lead you to the right decision, but indecision leads you nowhere.

With big decisions, you do need more information, however. With big decisions, you should consult with people, especially people who have been where you are and have been down that road before. With significant decisions, you gather input, you ponder the decision for a while, you weigh your options, and you don't make it until you have to, to give yourself time to evaluate all the possible scenarios that various decisions will generate. The only thing you don't ever want to do is make a decision that will take the company down, what we used to call "betting the farm." Don't make a big decision until you are very confident that you are making the right decision. And if you are not confident of a big decision, don't act.

A better approach would be to make a decision that doesn't have dire consequences, by finding a way to mitigate any problems. For example, in making acquisitions we would always say that we would rather walk away from 10 good deals than make one bad one. Always look at what the worst-case scenario might be and add a plan to deal with that if it should happen. If the worst case could significantly jeopardize the company, don't do it.

One way that we avoided having big decisions negatively impact the company was by trying new ideas on a small scale at first. For example, if someone had suggested we enter a new market, whether it be first aid or fire service, we would always buy one company in that business, staff it with one of our best people, and then test it out for a year or so. We could watch how it did and decide after several months whether it made sense to permanently add it to our product and service offerings. Some businesses we grew like crazy, often because they fit well with our existing services and customer base, and others we quickly got out of.

Retail dry-cleaning was one business that we were in for only about 18 months.

Many years ago, we made the decision to enter the retail dry-cleaning business. At the time, it made sense to us to extend services we were already offering, and retail dry-cleaning involved cleaning, which Cintas did, as well as route delivery, which we already had in place. It seemed like a natural outgrowth.

So, as with other big decisions, we set up one test location, which happened to be in Dallas, Texas, and after about a year, we knew that it had been a bad decision.

What we hadn't accounted for was that Cintas was a business-to-business (B2B) enterprise and retail dry-cleaning was business-to-consumer (B2C), with which we had no experience—nor did we really have an interest in moving into B2C. Our expertise was in the B2B sector, and we had been successful, in many cases, by being able to sell our existing customers on our new products and services. However, we couldn't do that with retail dry-cleaning; it just wasn't a natural extension.

After about 18 months, we sold the business, losing only a little money, because we had started small. Our worst-case scenario wasn't the end of the world.

When faced with a big decision and wanting to avoid making a big mistake, I always asked a lot of questions. Frequently, those questions sounded something like:

- "Why are you doing this?"
- "Why do you want to do this?"
- "Why does this make sense to you?"

- "Have you thought about this?"
- "Have you thought about that?"

I tried to assess the decision from all angles or to help other people do the same.

So if I had someone who was working for me come and ask me to bless a decision they were about to make, the first thing I would do is pepper them with questions. I wanted to be sure they had thoroughly researched their decision and evaluated all the angles. If I got good answers to my questions, I would assume that this was a person who usually did their homework and that their decision was likely based on solid research. And in that case, I would tell them to go right ahead.

But if I asked four or five questions and didn't get good answers, I would suspect that the individual hadn't really done their homework. Not being able to answer my questions told me that they were not as informed as they really should be before making a big decision, and I would often recommend that they go do some more investigating before I would approve their decision.

One of the best sources of input when making big decisions is people who have had to make similar decisions in the past, because people who have been where you are now know what you're thinking and feeling, and they may have evaluated many of the various alternatives you're evaluating. So before you make your decision, it would be wise to ask them about their decision-making process and any mistakes they made along the way. I think one of the best questions to ask someone whose advice you're seeking is "If you had to do it over again, what would you do differently?"

At Cintas, we always tried to avoid making mistakes. The best way we found to do that would be to turn to companies we respected who had more experience in certain areas, to learn from their experience. For example, when we decided to do more in-house training, we sought the advice of Motorola, which had established a whole university for their employees. We approached Motorola management about learning from their decisions, and they were more than willing to show us the ropes, so to speak.

We regularly stole ideas from other companies—not in an illegal way, but we would model our own decisions and strategies after those of companies that had been successful in similar endeavors. We were always looking for companies that were best-in-class and knew more about the decision in front of us than we did, and they became our role models. That's one way to avoid making mistakes: by using the knowledge and wisdom of people who are more experienced than you are.

Dick used to compliment me on my habit of seeking out the opinions of others. It just made sense to me to look for companies that were more successful or more experienced in a particular area and ask for their input or guidance. Many were more than willing to provide advice, especially if they were in a different industry. And yet I discovered that practice of seeking out role models was done way too infrequently.

I can recall a number of times, as a member of a board of directors, where the organization was about to embark on a new program or approach, and I'd ask, "Who is the best-in-class at this?" Or "Is there any other organization that has tried this?" Blank faces looking back at me around the table told me they hadn't looked.

Yet when we found companies who were the best in a particular area of business, whether it was training or logistics or onboarding new employees, we would ask to send a team to meet with and learn from them. Many were happy to do that, but so few companies ever ask, it seems. That's a lost opportunity to avoid making a mistake.

LOOK IN THE MIRROR BEFORE YOU LOOK OUT THE WINDOW

Of course, there will be plenty of times when things don't go as you had hoped—times when, despite your best efforts, the advice you received from others, the information you gathered, and the research you conducted, you won't achieve the desired results. It happens.

When something doesn't go right, it's important that you first look in the mirror at the person responsible: you. Don't try to place the blame elsewhere or look for scapegoats to save your reputation. No, look in the mirror and ask yourself, "What could I have done differently?" Then ask,

"Where did I fall down?" And, finally, "How am I going to avoid making this mistake again?"

The management members at Cintas frequently went through this exercise when an employee left. We would sit down as a team and ask ourselves, "Why did we lose this person?" And "Could we have done anything differently?" Sometimes we would realize where we had maybe misunderstood their priorities or where we had fallen down in building a relationship. But other times we would go through this exercise and realize that there really wasn't anything we could have done differently. Given the situation, the information we had, and the actions we took, we got the best result we could have.

As I said, mistakes happen, and not all of them are avoidable, unfortunately.

TRYING NEW THINGS DOESN'T ALWAYS LEAD TO MISTAKES

Mistakes are more likely to happen when you try something new, something where you have little background or experience. That's to be expected. But if you never try anything new, you'll never grow or advance. You have to be willing to try new things—and to let others try new things too.

As a manager, I routinely let people try things that, in many cases, I didn't agree with or that I didn't think had merit. If someone had an idea they were excited about and they'd done their research and wanted to explore it, as long as it wouldn't have significant negative financial or reputational consequences if they failed, I let them try it out. Showing that I believed in them and valued their input was more important than whether they succeeded or failed, in many cases.

A former employee of mine once told me that one of the reasons he enjoyed working for me so much was that I let him try things. Of course, I let him try things because I knew that was the only way he or the company was going to progress.

I remember years ago one of our partners came to my office with a new idea he wanted to share with me. At the time, Cintas was doing over $1 billion in entrance mat rentals, providing rubber mats that go on the floor at the front entrance of a building. Our employee proposed creating a "coffee mat," which would go on the floor in front of a coffee station in an office, where the coffee urn and mugs were placed on the counter, to catch spills and drips that made the floor sticky and dirty. The mat would have a little insignia with a steaming coffee cup, to indicate its purpose, he explained, creating an entirely new line of business.

My reaction? "That's the craziest idea I've ever heard. I don't know why you'd want to do that."

However, just because I personally thought it was crazy and a waste of time and money didn't mean it was a mistake. After all, mine was just one person's opinion, not based on research or information-gathering. So I told him if he wanted to, he could give it a try, to see whether he could rent them.

Within several months we had sales of $50,000 a week from those coffee mats. Clearly, my initial reaction was wrong. His was a good idea. But we never would have known that I was wrong unless I had let him try it. You need to let people try new things, and if they fail, they fail. But sometimes, they will succeed.

I truly believe that the level of innovation within an organization is based on management's willingness to let people try new things. Stifling ideas certainly doesn't move a company forward. And you can argue internally about whether an idea will work, but until you actually try it and give it a chance, you'll never know. In the case of the coffee mats, Cintas would have missed out on millions of dollars in revenue from that one simple idea if we had been unwilling to explore new opportunities. We were willing to fail and to make mistakes, and in doing so, we discovered new products and markets we couldn't have predicted.

Avoiding mistakes may help you have fewer failures, but you'll also have fewer breakthroughs and successes. You have to be willing to look for improvement opportunities, or what we called positive discontent. If you're always looking for ways to be better, never resting on your laurels, you'll progress further and faster than companies that are satisfied with where they are.

Now, it's important to avoid negative discontent, or constant complaining about what's not going right, and to focus instead on solutions to problems or weaknesses that you identify. If you're always on alert for new opportunities and are willing to take small risks, you'll get further in your career—and your company will grow faster—than if you never put yourself in a position to stumble.

CHAPTER SUMMARY

- Mistakes aren't bad, even though people try hard to avoid them. Mistakes are a sign that you tried something new, which is how individuals and companies progress and gain new skills and capabilities.

- When making small decisions, many people attempt to gather all of the information possible in order to avoid a mistake. Yet, with insignificant decisions, that's a waste of time and effort. A better approach is to shoot for 70 or 80 percent of the information you need and then make a choice.

- With big decisions, however, gathering input from experienced sources is always smart. Conduct research, ask for opinions, and seek out experienced sources to learn what they would have done differently, if anything, knowing what they know now. And when you are not confident as to what you should do, don't act.

- Turn to best-in-class organizations for guidance when exploring new initiatives. Many are more than willing to share their expertise as long as you aren't a direct competitor. This can be an extremely useful source of information that can also help you avoid making mistakes. Learn from theirs.

- Innovation is the result of a willingness to explore and try new ideas. The more willing a company is to let its employees pursue new ideas, the more advances it will make.

CHAPTER 11

HAVING HIGH EXPECTATIONS

There's nothing more important when managing people or running a business than having high expectations of them and of yourself.

Think back to the people who, in your own life, helped you to do your best work—to be better than you ever thought you could be. You may recall a teacher, or a coach, or a boss, but whoever it is, it's likely you'll picture someone who helped you believe in yourself and pushed you to accomplish things you didn't think you were capable of. They are the people who had high expectations of you.

BEING A MOTIVATOR FOR OTHERS

A book I read recently had a quote that resonated with me: "The road to success is always under construction." That rang true to me because there will always be obstacles or road bumps to your success; they are a given. But the people around you can help you get over and past those obstacles. They help get you over those bumps. Sometimes they encourage you as you encounter those bumps, sometimes they push you over them or drag you, or sometimes they may yell at you to get you over those bumps—but somehow you manage to get over those bumps. Looking back, you may even decide that overcoming them wasn't so hard: "I can do that," you remind yourself.

You know you can do it, whatever "it" is, because you have a support system around you that is committed to your success.

Now, those people who pushed you—maybe kicking and screaming—to do your best work may not be your favorite people. Even as you appreciate their methods to help you achieve, you may not want to hang out with them socially or grab a beer with them after work. Some of those people who love and support you in their own way are taskmasters; they're demanding. And you may not always want to be in their presence for that reason.

Despite any reluctance you may feel about spending time with them socially, they're among your biggest cheerleaders. That is, they have high expectations for you.

Having high expectations of others is absolutely critical for any person who manages or leads other people. You need to be able to recognize what others are capable of, to convey that confidence in them to them, and then to find what type of support works best at helping them to do their very best. You need to expect people to be as good as—or even better than—you are.

Just as others expected more from you, now it's your turn to do that for the people who work for you. You need to have high expectations of those who report to you and to let them know you're confident in their ability to achieve more. Give them your confidence, so that they will work to exceed their own expectations.

GOAL-SETTING BASICS

I've always said that expectations, which are a lot like goals, should be measurable, should be achievable, and should tie into the company's overall goals. You don't want an employee to have a goal that doesn't help accomplish the overall objectives of the organization and that isn't achievable or measurable.

So many people have goals or expectations to improve some aspect of their performance. What does that mean? What does "improvement" look like? Is a 1 percent improvement an achievement?

No, you need to be able to monitor to what degree improvement was made and on a particular timetable. One way to frame an expectation is to take a particular measure, whether it's injuries on the job or weekly sales or customer accolades, from point A to point B by a certain date. For example, you might tell a manager that you want them to reduce partner turnover for their team: "I want you to reduce partner turnover for your group from 10 percent to 7 percent within the next year."

That's an expectation, and it gives them a specific target to work toward. You never want to get to the end of the month or the quarter or the year and not be clear whether an expectation has been met.

Of course, sometimes there are external factors that impact their ability to perform, such as a sudden economic downturn or a fire at the plant, for which you have to make exceptions. However, you always need to set the bar high, but within reach.

SETTING A HIGH BAR

A number of years ago, Jim Collins, the author of *Good to Great*, spoke at our annual management meeting at Cintas, and he told us, "Great companies and great managers have a feeling that you can delight me, but you can never satisfy me." I think that people who have high expectations have that same outlook; they're never satisfied. I don't mean that in a bad way, that they're dissatisfied, but that they recognize that it's always possible to improve.

For that reason, you should never be satisfied with your own performance or with that of your subordinates or your peers or your organization. You can always do better. And the day that you are satisfied is the day that you stop getting better. The day that anyone's performance is good enough—it's satisfactory—is the day that you stop striving to improve. And it's all downhill from there.

Now, that doesn't mean that you shouldn't praise people when they do something well, when they excel and exceed your expectations. In fact, praise motivates people much more than reprimanding them does. You should always give kudos and compliments when someone performs at a high level. Tell them immediately, recognize them repeatedly, preferably in front of their peers. Great leaders let people know when they do a good job.

However, after complimenting the heck out of them for their great performance, great leaders also then ask, "Now, how can we do better?" That takes nothing away from the terrific thing they just did, but asking how to continue to improve also helps people self-assess and evaluate what they would have to do differently if they wanted even slightly better results. Getting into the habit of regularly assessing your performance, and that of the people around you, can help you spot opportunities to get even a 1 percent improvement. Over time, those tiny 1 percent improvements can really add up.

The art of developing people is to learn how to constantly stretch them but never break them. I learned that from my father, who once gave a speech and said, "The art of being a good parent is teaching your kids discipline, without breaking their will." I think the same is true of developing employees.

Dick helped me do things I didn't initially think I was capable of. When I became CEO of the company, he sat down with me and told me, "Bob, I think you're going to be a better CEO than I've been."

Surprised, I asked him, "Why would you say that, Dick? I think you've done an unbelievable job!"

"Well, the company's getting bigger," he explained, "and one of your strengths is evaluating and choosing from all of the many possible strategies for growth that are in front of us. You're a skilled strategic thinker. You're going to be great!"

Honestly, I don't know whether Dick really believed that about me, but what he was trying to do was give me the encouragement and confidence to be able to do the job well. Following in his footsteps was not an easy thing to do, and he probably realized that. He was renowned in Cincinnati and the catalyst to building one of the greatest companies I've ever known. But in that moment, he was trying to motivate me.

Sure, there were other times when Dick would call me in his office and split me right up the middle for something I'd done or for something he didn't think was the right thing to do. But he would always put me back together before I left his office. And if he was concerned that he'd been too harsh with me, the next day he would call me back in to check on me, saying something to the effect of "Bob, I know I was tough on you yesterday, but I did that to help you. I did that to make you better."

Some people talk about the sandwich approach to managing people or communicating with people. With that, you have two pieces of bread and a piece of meat in the middle. The first piece of bread is a positive expression of some kind, such as, "Bob, you're doing a wonderful job, and I think the world of you." It's followed by some meaty statement that may make you stop and think, such as, "However, you've really messed this situation up right here. I wouldn't have approached it that way at all." And then the last piece of bread is encouragement, such as, "But I have total confidence that you can fix that problem and that you'll do great things from here on out."

It's important to be able to identify how and when to be tough— when the situation calls for a pat you on the back versus a kick in the rear. A good boss, or a good manager, knows when to do which. They have high expectations of themselves and of those who work for and with them.

BEING REALISTIC

It's important that those expectations you set be realistic, based on past performance, rather than idealistic or unreasonable. Yes, you need to set a high bar for the performance level you expect others to achieve, but if they've never come close to that in the past, you're only setting them up for disappointment and failure if the bar is out of reach. That's not fair. Your expectations need to be achievable, but you should push them to exert extra effort. If you set expectations that are clearly impossible from the start, you'll get nowhere. Your employees won't exert any effort at all because the outcome is a foregone conclusion—meaning failure.

For example, asking a salesperson to generate sales of $500,000 this quarter when they've consistently sold $200,000 to $250,000 is useless, unless you're intending to invest a significant amount of new resources to help boost their performance. It's a lot like asking an athlete, a sprinter, for example, to beat their personal best by several seconds this season, simply because you asked them to. It's one thing to push them to shave time off their own record with new exercises or drills, but you can't wish improved performance out of thin air. It needs to be based in reality on past performance and fueled by encouragement and new tools or resources.

You need to give a lot of thought as to what you're asking people to do and what it would take for them to be successful.

I think back on 2003, when Scott Farmer succeeded me as CEO at Cintas, and how the US economy started to nosedive only a couple years later and how there were some internal issues the company had to address at the same time. We had a couple of mediocre years in a row, and I pushed Scott hard to try to figure out how to turn things around. I was on him as if he had control over what was happening, when, I realized soon thereafter, he really didn't.

I called him into my office one day to explain to him, "Scott, I've been really tough on you the last couple of years because the company hasn't been performing as well as I had expected.

"But in looking back on all the obstacles you had to face, I don't think I could have done any better," I told him. "You did a fine job."

Sometimes you do set expectations too high, and it's important to communicate your mistake as soon as you recognize it. But I would rather see people aim too high than too low.

In some cases, you may believe that you've set a stretch goal—one that is attainable but that will require extra effort—for an employee, and they may perceive it as totally unrealistic. In that case, you need to explain why you know they're capable, to motivate and encourage them toward achieving that goal. Otherwise, they may give up.

BUILDING NEW SKILLS

I faced this firsthand early in my career, when Dick went to Cleveland to start to grow what was then a very small company. I was a 24-year-old employee. He made me general manager of the company he had poured his heart into, which made me nervous from the start. What made me even more nervous was one of the goals that he had set for me, which was to land the Kroger account in Dayton, Ohio. We were doing business with Kroger in Cincinnati, but we didn't have the Dayton account yet, and Dick wanted me to sell it.

Given that I had never sold anything in my life and had never been a salesman, I was a little perplexed by this goal. It seemed out of reach for me. So I asked him, "Dick, I don't understand this. Are you saying that even if I make all of my sales numbers and profit percentage and all of my other goals, you're telling me that you won't be happy with me if I don't sell one particular customer?"

"Yes," he said, to my surprise.

I went home that night feeling sorry for myself, complaining that I had been given what I believed was an unattainable goal. It was unrealistic, and his expectation just didn't seem fair. How in the world was I going to sell Kroger? I asked myself. I'd never sold anything. I wasn't a salesperson.

But I didn't have a choice. I had to sell the Dayton Kroger on using Cintas.

Honestly, I didn't know what I was doing, but I remember going to Dayton to talk to the purchasing agent at Kroger to find out what I could do to get their account. The agent told me, "We're very happy with our current supplier, and I don't know that we would even consider changing." That conversation did not inspire confidence.

Unsure of what to do after that, I went back to Dick to ask his advice. "What do I do now, Dick? They don't want to switch."

"What do you do?" he asked. "What you do is get in your car and drive around to the Kroger stores, and you ask to speak with the manager. And you ask each manager about the service they're getting, whether they're happy, and what could be done better."

That's exactly what I did. I drove around Dayton, Ohio, for about a week, visiting just about every Kroger store in that town, which numbered around 20, talking to every manager and taking copious notes about what they told me. Then I called the purchasing agent back and asked to meet with him again. Although he was resistant at first, unsure of why he should give me more of his time, he finally agreed.

However, when we met and I told him what I had done, he was madder than a hornet. "I didn't tell you that you could go around and meet with our managers," he said angrily.

"But, sir, let me tell you what those managers told me." And then I started rattling off all the things the managers revealed. He was very interested in what I had to share.

"Look, those managers don't want to call the corporate office and complain to you," I told him. "But when I asked them a few questions, here's what they told me. I know you think you're happy with your current supplier, because you're not hearing any complaints, but if you call and talk to your store managers, they'll tell you they're not happy."

And I managed to sell Kroger in Dayton on Cintas's services.

Looking back, I see what Dick was trying to do for me. He knew that I had never sold anything, and he knew that being able to sell would be critical for my success as a leader, so he pushed me to get that experience firsthand. He wanted me to understand what it felt like to sell a customer, but he was also willing to help me and guide me, to improve my odds of success. I couldn't have done it without his suggestion to talk to the store managers, but after I implemented that idea with success, I realized that selling wasn't so hard. Dick helped me over that hump, to see that I was capable even when I was unsure initially. Eventually, I got to the point where I believed I could sell anyone just about anything.

Setting the bar high, and then adjusting it higher, is what having high expectations looks like. It's what great leaders do routinely for their direct reports, and it's what I tried to do for mine.

I remember one time I gave an employee an assignment, and he finished it and presented it to me proudly, telling me, "Here, let me show you what I did." I went through it, and I told him, "Well, this is good, but it's not good enough."

You would have thought I had cut his heart out. He said, "What do you mean it's not good enough?"

So I showed him, "Here's what you should have done. This isn't bad, but you can do better than this. I'd suggest that when you finish something and you think it's really good, step back from it for a day or two, then look at it again with fresh eyes and ask yourself, 'How can I make it better?'"

He went away, worked on it some more, and then came back to me a few weeks later and said, "You know what? You're right." He was able to significantly improve it because I told him I knew he could. Once he was confident that he could make it better, he found a way to do just that.

It all comes down to motivation. Great leaders are able to motivate the people who work for them to give it their all, to do their best work and then find a way to improve it even more. If you motivate them properly, they'll do whatever it takes. They'll work unbelievable hours, try a million different approaches, and keep trying to improve if you push and stretch them. And when they're down, you need to be there to pick them up and dust them off. There's nothing more important than motivating people to do their best work and having high expectations for them by helping them to be better employees. They can't do that on their own.

I remember being on the board of a university and struggling with what to do about an employee who wasn't performing to expectations, so they let that person go and hired a replacement. Soon after the new individual started, I was meeting with the president, who was telling me what a terrific job this new employee was doing. "She's off to a great start," he told me, and "she's already done this and that and the other thing," marveling at what a fantastic job she was doing.

"Do you know why the last person didn't do those things?" I asked him.

He looked at me like a deer in headlights. "No, why?" he asked me.

"Because you allowed it," I told him. "You didn't expect the last person in that position to do the things that their replacement is now, so they didn't," I told him. "If you had expected this of your last employee, and told them what you expected and when you needed it done, they would have performed just as well. They would have done all these things that the new hire is doing. It wasn't their fault that they didn't perform; it was yours." The look in his eyes told me he knew I was right.

Have high expectations for yourself and for those around you, keeping in mind that you may need to adjust those expectations based on the experience level of the individual you're working with. Ken Blanchard, author of a number of books, including *Leading at a Higher Level*, used to explain that it's important to praise "enthusiastic beginners" for doing something approximately right. The idea was that if you encourage them, they'll continue to try to improve. But if you criticize their early efforts, they'll shut down and stop performing altogether. Better to treat everyone as enthusiastic beginners.

CHAPTER SUMMARY

- Think about who in your life got the most out of you and strive to push those around you to improve performance the same way, ideally through encouragement.
- The art of developing people is to learn how to constantly stretch them and push them—but not break them. That means setting expectations that are measurable and achievable and that tie into the organization's larger goals.
- Never be satisfied with your own, or anyone else's, initial efforts. Encourage them to take another look or another approach to their task if you know they can do better.
- Most importantly, express your confidence in them. Remind them that you know they can do what you're asking, that you would never give them an impossible task.

EPILOGUE

Any time you have an opportunity to make a difference in this world and you don't, then you are wasting your time on Earth.
—Roberto Clemente, professional baseball player

I consider myself very fortunate to have spent 50 years with one company, from which I retired four years ago. When I retired, I asked myself, "Now what are you going to do? What are you going to focus on for the rest of your life?"

I'm not the kind of person who can be a couch potato, sitting and watching television all day; I've never been that kind of person. I can't sit still and do nothing for long. So I reflected on the quote above by Roberto Clemente, which has become somewhat of a guide in my life.

When I pass from this earth and face my maker, I know he's not going to ask me how many cars or boats I had, how many homes I owned, how many friends I had, or how much money I made. He's going to ask one question: "What have you done for the people you left behind?"

I've always felt that I should arrive prepared with a good answer to that question.

So, since retiring, I've spent a fair amount of time thinking about how I could best give back. I believe it's very important for people like me, who have had wonderful opportunities like I've had and learned what I've learned, to give back—to give of my time and treasure.

GIVE YOUR TIME

One way I've tried to do that is through mentoring. I've mentored a number of people during my career, some of whom still call me from time to time to get my thoughts or advice on a tough decision they might be facing. "What do you think I should do, Bob?" they'll ask me. I get calls like that every week or two from someone, and I'm happy to take them.

Sometimes the people on the other end of the line are businesspeople, and other times they are people I mentored at Xavier. I had the pleasure of getting to know the former center of the women's basketball team during her four years at the university, for example. We've stayed in touch, and she calls me every now and then to get my take on a particular situation or my opinion on a decision she's about to make. I enjoy the chance to have those discussions.

Just last week I received a call from a former Xavier basketball player. He spent only one year there, but during that time we got to know one another well. We've stayed in touch, and on his last call to me, he expressed an interest in investing in real estate and wanted to know what I thought about the idea. He lives in Indianapolis but was considering buying residential real estate near the Xavier campus, to rent out to Xavier students. So I asked him, "Why would you want to buy in Cincinnati? Why not invest where you live? Butler is probably the biggest university in Indianapolis, so why not start there?" I suggested.

Then I asked, "Have you ever invested in residential real estate?" He said no, he hadn't, so I told him that I knew two people who had done what he was talking about and I asked if they could call him to share what they'd learned, what to look for, and how to be successful. He was happy to have that counsel. I make those kinds of connections regularly, and I enjoy it, because I feel like I'm helping both people out through networking.

I also look to share what I've learned with area nonprofit boards that I've served on. I've always been on at least one, because my time was limited by work, but even then, I felt like my knowledge and expertise might be useful, to help the nonprofit be more successful. And I was happy to be a part of that success.

Of course, nonprofit organizations are completely different from for-profit corporations. They aren't businesses, and many of the people who work there are volunteers, so you can't instruct them to do something, as you could as a CEO, but instead you have to motivate them. I always tried to motivate, not demand.

GIVE YOUR TREASURE

In addition to giving of your time, I think it's also important to share your treasure. I haven't given away everything I own, but I've tried to be generous through the years, to share the bounty that I've been given. I've tried to be a role model to my children, too, to show them how they can have maximum impact with their donations.

My approach has been to give fewer nonprofits a larger share of my treasure. For example, rather than giving away, say, $50,000 to 50 different nonprofits, a better approach would be to give $15,000 to three organizations and then spread the remaining $5,000 over several more. It's hard to have a significant impact with a few hundred dollars here and there, though every little donation does have the potential to do good work.

However, my recommendation to my children, which I also share with you, is to pick one or two organizations or nonprofits that you feel strongly about, ones where you support the work they're doing and how they're doing it. Then focus your time and your treasure there.

SHARING VALUES

One way I have tried to convey this idea to my family was through regular meetings with them. When they reached their 30s, we began having quarterly meetings about the impact we wanted to have as a family and as individuals. We started by coming up with a family mission statement, and I began sharing many of the quotes and sayings I'd heard that had impacted my life. I told them, "When I'm dead and gone, if you want to get a sense of what I would have said or thought, you can look at this piece of paper and you'll know what I would do. Whether you read these ideas and sayings is up to you, but it will be here if you ever want to know what I think."

During our quarterly family meetings, I would talk with them about my estate, my estate plan, why I came up with the plan I did, how they fit into it, what their role is in preserving the things that we've set up. At the core of these discussions are our family values. I think it's a whole lot easier to pass down wealth than it is to pass down values, which is why creating our family mission statement was such an important first step. It keeps us aligned as far as the bigger picture regarding the positive impact we want to make on the world.

I tried to start sharing my values when my three kids were younger, mainly by posing situations and asking them questions. For example, at the dinner table, I might ask, "If you could vote, who would get your vote for president? And why?" Then we'd go around the table, and each child would say who had their vote and why, and I would ask follow-up questions, such as, "Well, what do you think about their policy about this? Or have you thought about that?" I wouldn't tell them who my candidate was because I wanted them to think critically about the big issues. We did that regularly, and I hope it gave them an idea of how I'd want them to think and act.

Finding activities we all enjoyed as a family was one way that forged the bonds we have today, which have kept us close. Although I certainly never neglected my family during my career, I did work a lot. That meant that I missed a lot of soccer games and baseball games and other events because I was traveling for work. I wanted to be there, but I couldn't always, unfortunately. So I needed to find other ways to make sure that my wife and children knew how much I loved and appreciated them.

MAKING A DIFFERENCE

Once I retired, I saw the opportunity to shift my focus to my family. I'm so blessed to have wonderful children who all have respect for each other and for me. It's mutual respect. We talk openly about everything, and although we may not agree on everything, that isn't as important as talking about the issues.

I want to be sure that I share all the knowledge and experience that I've been so blessed to have. I don't want to take it to the grave with me. I don't think that's what God wants me to do, to hoard it. I think he'd rather that I impart all that I've learned to as many people as possible. That was a significant motivator for me to write this book:

so that when I arrive at the pearly gates, I'll have many stories to tell of how I tried to make the lives of others better. That continues to be my fervent hope.

ENDNOTES

1. Brower, Marvin, *The Will to Manage: Corporate Success through Programmed Management*, McGraw-Hill: New York, 1966, p. 16.
2. Bureau Labor Statistics: https://www.bls.gov/news.release/jolts.t16.htm.

ABOUT THE AUTHOR

ROBERT J. KOHLHEPP

BORN:
Covington, Kentucky, U.S.A.

EDUCATION:
B.S. Business Administration – Thomas More College – 1963
M.B.A. – Xavier University – 1971

BUSINESS:
Retired Chairman – Cintas Corporation

Joined Cintas in July, 1967, as Controller. Promoted to positions of General Manager, Vice President and Treasurer. In 1979 elected Executive Vice President and a member of the company's Board of Directors. In 1984 elected President and in 1995 elected Chief Executive Officer. Served as Vice Chairman from 2003 to 2009 and as Chairman of the Board from 2009-2016

Member – Chief Executives Organization
Member – World Presidents' Organization
Member – Commercial Club – Cincinnati, Ohio
Member – Commonwealth Club – Cincinnati, Ohio

Certified Public Accountant (Inactive)

Past Member – Business Advisory Council – Xavier University
Past Member – Cincinnati Chapter – Young President's Organization

DIRECTOR/TRUSTEE:

Horizon Community Funds – Covington, KY – Board of Trustees

PAST DIRECTOR/TRUSTEE:

Cintas Corporation – Cincinnati, Ohio – Chairman of the Board
Eagle Hospitality Properties Trust -- Covington, KY -- Director
Mead Corporation – Dayton, Ohio – Director
United Way & Community Chest – Cincinnati, Ohio – Trustee
Cincinnati Association for The Blind – Cincinnati, Ohio – Trustee
Uniform & Textile Service Association (International Industry Trade Assn.) – Director
Parker Hannifin Corporation -- Cleveland, Ohio – Lead Director
Tosca Corporation – Atlanta, Georgia – Director
Xavier University – Cincinnati, Ohio – Board of Trustees

MARRIED:

Linda (nee Meyers) – 1968
Three children

INDEX

A

Answers, defining in hiring process, 66–67
Appearance, professional, 18–19
Atomic Habits (Clear), 3

B

Behavior (past), examining in hiring process, 62–63
Blanchard, Ken, *Leading at a Higher Level*, 144
Blockers, 85
Boundaries, setting, 50–52
Brower, Marvin, *The Will to Manage: Corporate Success through Programmed Management*, 32–33
Built to Last (Collins), 9
Business affairs, separating from personal affairs, 47–49

C

Candidates (job)
    eliminating lukewarm, 68
    finding the right, 69
Capital provision, as a management system process, 33
Chrysler, 42–43
Cintas
    competitive urgency, 29–30
    conflicts of interest, 53–56
    constituents of, 13
    corporate character, 17–30
    cultlike culture, 9–11
    culture fit, 3–5
    culture shock, 7–8
    customer satisfaction, 26–27
    decision-making, 128–131
    employee turnover, 87–88
    honesty at, 47
    importance of principal objective at, 13–14
    innovation at, 132–134
    "look in the mirror" exercise, 131–132
    making things right, 52–53
    management systems, 31–44
    Meticulous Hiring Process, 57, 60–68, 69, 71
    operations manual, 33–35
    partner communication, 22–26
    partner safety, 21–22
    Partners Plan, 12
    performance reviews, 73–76
    policy committee, 38
    principal objective, 5–6
    reinforcing feedback, 120–125
    respect for partners, 27–29
    Safety and Improvement Committee, 21
    Scott Farmer and, 140
    setting boundaries, 50–52
    succession planning, 82–84
    trucks and professionalism, 19–21
    workforce diversity, 70–71
Cleanliness, and professionalism, 19–20

Clear, James, *Atomic Habits,* 3
Clemente, Roberto, 112
Collins, Jim, 3, 9, 137
Communication
  of leaders, 107–108
  with partners, 22–26
Company philosophy, as a
  management system process, 32
Company policy
  establishing, as a management
    system process, 32
  ethics and violations, 50
Competitive advantage, culture as,
  41–44
Competitive urgency, 29–30
Confidence, of leaders, 110–111
Conflicts of interest, eliminating,
  53–56
Consistency, importance of, 31, 40–41
Constituents, importance of, 6–7. See
  also *specific constituents*
Control information, as a management
  system process, 33
Corporate character, defining your,
  17–30
Courtesy, in corporate character, 28
Cultlike culture, fostering, 9–11
Culture
  about, 1
  as competitive advantage, 41–44
  cultlike, 9–11
  determining compatibility, 67–68
  storytelling and, 8–9
Culture shock, handling, 7–8
Customers
  as constituents, 6–7, 13
  satisfaction of, 26–27

D
Decision-making, 127–131
Detzel, Joe, 4
Directness, in corporate character, 28

Diversity, of workforce, 70–71
Dow Chemical, 54–55
Dress code, and professionalism, 18–19
Drucker, Peter, 29

E
Edison, Thomas, 110
Effectiveness, of feedback, 117–119
Einstein, Isaac, 109
Employees. *See* Partners
Enron, 13
Enthusiasm, of leaders, 110–111
Enthusiastic beginners, 144
Ethics
  about, 45–46
  eliminating conflicts of interest,
    53–56
  honesty, 46–47
  making things right, 52–53
  separating business and personal
    affairs, 47–49
  setting boundaries, 50–52
  standards in corporate character,
    28–29
Expectations
  being a motivator, 135–136
  being realistic, 139–140
  building new skills, 140–144
  goal-setting, 136–137
  of leaders, 111–112
  setting a high bar, 137–139

F
Facilities provision, as a management
  system process, 33
Fair find approach, 119
Farmer, Dick
  on competitive urgency, 29
  on conflicts of interest, 54–55
  on cultlike culture, 10
  on differences of opinion, 81
  on "fair find approach," 119

leadership qualities of, 106, 107
on management systems, 31–32
on principal objective, 3–4
on separating business and personal
    affairs, 47–48
on setting expectations, 138–143
The Spirit Is the Difference, 4, 8
on "taking their temperature,"
    90–91
on visionaries, 102–103
Farmer, Scott, 140
Feedback
    defined, 116
    fair find approach, 119
    honesty in, 116–117
    necessity of, 112
    performance reviews, 73–76
    providing detailed, 78–79
    providing effective, 117–119
    reinforcing, 120–125
    timing for, 79–80
    trust and, 120
Firestone, 52–53
Flexibility, of leaders, 109–110
Florida A&M, 70
Followers, leaders' attractiveness to,
    105–106

G

GE assessment model, 83
General Electric (GE), 83, 87, 88–89
Generosity, 147
Giving back, 145–149
Goals
    basics of setting, 136–137
    establishing, as a management
        system process, 32
    in performance reviews, 75–76
Good to Great (Collins), 3, 137
Green Bay Packers, 104
Gut check, 51

H

Hawkins, Bill, 36, 37
Hiring process
    asking pointed questions, 63–64
    conducting multiple interviews, 61
    defining answers, 66–67
    eliminating lukewarm candidates,
        68
    examining past behavior, 62–63
    finding the right candidate, 69
    hiring the right people, 59–72
    leveraging human resources
        information, 81–82
    meticulous hiring, 60–68
    "must-haves," 61–62
    "preferreds," 61–62
Hoff, Jim, 103
Honesty
    and ethics, 46–47
    in feedback, 116–117
    of leaders, 112
Hoyt, Dave, 35, 36
Human resources information,
    leveraging, 81–82

I

Iacocca, Lee, 42–43
Image business, 18–19
Improvement opportunities, in
    performance reviews, 75, 76
Innovation, mistakes and, 132–134
Insanity, 109
Integrity, of leaders, 112
Interpretation, danger of, 35–37
Interviews, conducting multiple, 61

J

Job performance, in performance
    reviews, 75
Jobs, hiring for. *See* Hiring process

K

Keller, Gary, *The One Thing*, 3
Kohlhepp, Robert J., 4, 36, 47–48, 54–55, 81, 151–152
Kroc, Ray, 40–41
Kroger, 141–142

L

Leadership
    about, 99
    characteristics of great leaders, 101–113
    communication, 107–108
    confidence, 110–111
    enthusiasm, 110–111
    expectations of leaders, 111–112
    flexibility, 109–110
    honesty, 112
    integrity, 112
    motivators, 104–105
    respect, 108–109
    standards, 111–112
    trust, 108–109
    visionaries, 101–103
Leading at a Higher Level (Blanchard), 144
Learning, from mistakes, 127–134
Legality, ethics and, 50
Lehman Brothers, 13
L.L. Bean, 18
Lombardi, Vince, 104
"Look in the mirror" exercise, 131–132

M

Management, defined, 32
Management systems
    culture as competitive advantage, 41–44
    dynamic, 37–40
    establishing, 31–44
    importance of consistency, 40–41
McDonald's, 40–41

Mentoring, as giving back, 146–147
Meticulous hiring, 60–68
Miller, Bill, 4
Mistakes, learning from, 127–134
Money, giving your, 147
Moral standards, in corporate character, 28–29
Motivators
being, 135–136
leaders as, 104–105
Motorola, 130
"Must-haves," in hiring process, 61–62

N

National Black MBA Association, 70
Nonprofit organizations, giving money/time to, 146–147

O

Objective-setting, as a management system process, 32
The One Thing (Keller), 3
Open-door policy, 23
Opinion, differences in, 80–81
Organizational structure plan, as a management system process, 32

P

Partners
    about, 57
    activating, as a management system process, 33
    blockers, 85
    communication with, 22–26
    as constituents, 6–7, 13
    differences of opinion, 80–81
    employee turnover, 87–88
    evaluating, 88–89
    hiring the right, 59–72
    holding on to your best, 87–97
    keeping the door open for, 95–96
    leveraging human resources information, 81–82

managing effectively, 73–86
meticulous hiring, 60–68
overall rating, 76–78
performance reviews, 73–76
professional development planning, 84–85
providing detailed feedback, 78–79
respect for, 27–29
rewarding, 12
safety of, 21–22
succession planning, 82–84
"taking their temperature," 89–93
timing for feedback, 79–80
People. *See* Partners
Performance reviews, 73–76. *See also* Feedback
Personal affairs, separating from business affairs, 47–49
Personnel, as a management system process, 33
Pointed questions, asking during hiring process, 63–64
Positive discontent, 29
"Preferreds," in hiring process, 61–62
Principal objective
    companies without a, 15
    determining your, 3–15
    developing an effective, 13–15
Procedures, establishing as a management system process, 33
Procter & Gamble, 41, 64
Professional development planning, 84–85
Professionalism, corporate character and, 18–21
Prospanica, 70

R

Realistic expectations, 139–140
References, checking, 64–65
Respect
    of leaders, 108–109
    mutual, 148–149
Rewarding partners, 12
Rotte, Bruce, 12

S

Safety
    and ethics, 51
    of partners, 21–22
Safety and Improvement Committee (Cintas), 21
Shareholders, as constituents, 6–7, 13
Skill-building, 140–144
Social Security, 40
The Spirit Is the Difference (Farmer), 4, 8
Standards
    of leaders, 111–112
    setting, as a management system process, 33
Storytelling, 8–9
Strategy planning, as a management system process, 32
"Stress questions," asking, 65–66
Succession planning, 82–84
Summitt, Pat, 59

T

"Taking their temperature," 89–93
Tesla, 18
Time, giving your, 146–147
Toughness, 115–116. *See also* Feedback
Trust
    and feedback, 120
    of leaders, 108–109
Turnover, employee, 87–88
Tyco, 47

U

University of Connecticut (UConn), 59
University of Tennessee, 59
UPS standard, 19

V
Values, sharing, 147–148
Visionaries, leaders as, 101–103

W
Walmart, 109
Walton, Sam, 109
*The Will to Manage: Corporate Success
through Programmed Management*
(Brower), 32–33
Workforce. *See* Partners

X
Xavier University, 66, 103, 146

Z
Zappos, 18